SPREAD LOVE
(and buttercream!)

Sharing is caring!

We'd love to see your enthusiasm and excitement for the book! Whether you post pictures of the book, share a quote you found powerful, or fill your feed with photo documentation of your beautiful creations using our recipes, we'd love to see them! Please tag us on social media so we can show you some love in return!

 @Thèm de la Crème

 @themdelacreme

SPREAD
LOVE
(and buttercream!)

Recipes & reflections where love is the
first ingredient and a sweeter world
is ours for the baking

Coltan J. Schoenike

WITH CONTRIBUTION BY **MARIA CAULEY**

thèm
de la crème

A THÈM DE LA CRÈME BOOK · MENOMONIE, WI

Love is like
a cup of sugar.
If you run out
of your own,
someone else
might have some
for you.

Acknowledgments

Jacob,

Thank you for always being there for me no matter what. Of course, this is including-but-not-limited-to whenever I have my crazy, spur-of-the-moment ideas, like this book. Among the many reasons I'm so in love with you, I can't complain about how you always let me bake for you and spoil you with affection and baked goods. I love you always.

My mom, dad, and sister,

Thank you for encouraging the million-and-a-half creative endeavors in my life and keeping a good poker face during cards or when I'd tell you about the next unexpected plot twist of life. And of course, all good baking starts with learning in the kitchen from your mom.

Grace and Zen,

Thank you for all of your creative input at every stage of Thèm de la Crème, always being ready for brainstorming new flavors!

Alexa and Makenzie,

Thank you for always being willing to taste-test the next new flavors and help me hone my craft. You'll always be my guinea pigs and my original hype girls.

Julian and Olivia,

Thank you for your eternal wisdom and experience that made the process of self-publishing way less of a herculean effort than it could have been. What would I do without you?

Markie,

Thank you for the countless ways that you've fostered my growth over the years and profoundly impacted my ability to become the person I am now. I'll never be able to truly quantify the gifts you've given me or thank you enough for them.

and last but certainly not least...

I give my profound thanks to the communities that have and continue to support me and this endeavor of positively contributing to the world. This includes my friends and chosen family in the queer and transgender communities, as well as the many great people I've come to know in my Menomonie, Wisconsin community.

Because community is so important to me, many of those very same friends and loved ones have left their marks within this book, and for that I am eternally grateful.

Thank you all, you truly are the sweetest!

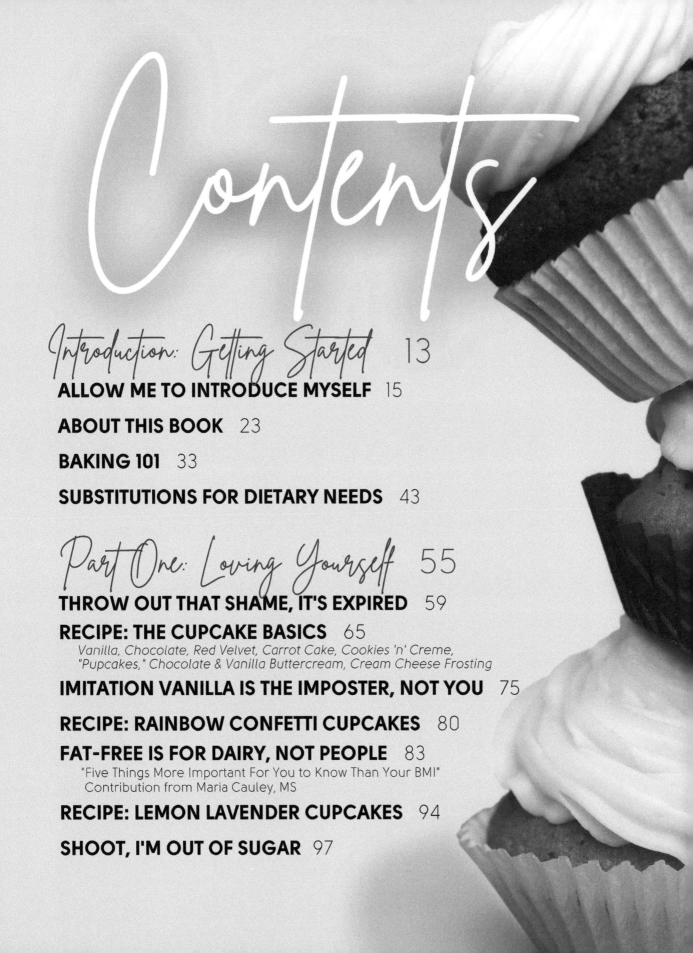

Contents

Introduction

GETTING STARTED

Growing up, my mom had bleeding
hearts in her garden.

I love how they open up as they grow.
I think we could learn from them.

My mom was also the one who taught me all
she knows about baking and using your oven
to bring happiness everywhere you go.

Thanks Mom.

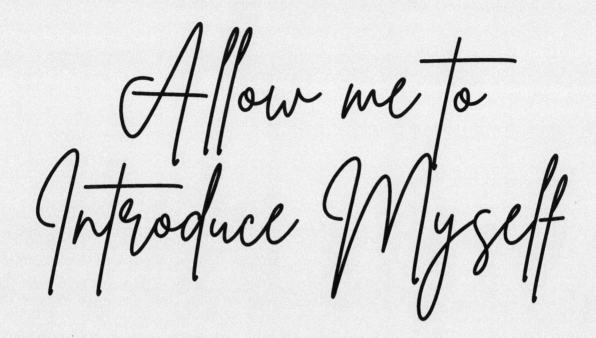

Allow me to Introduce Myself

Coltan J. Schoenike, MS
they, them, theirs

Oh god, it's that part where I talk about myself. It's that midwestern part of me where someone is like, "Hey, want to tell us about who you are?" and your brain just shuts down and all you can see is that "ERROR 404 NOT FOUND" screen or the little dinosaur game you can play on your web browser when you have no internet connection.

Well, I guess we can start with the basics? Um, hi everybody, my name is Coltan Schoenike and my pronouns are they, them, theirs. I'm the author of this book. I also have a Master's Degree in Marriage and Family Therapy and bake an obscene amount of cupcakes on a regular basis.

Okay, that wasn't so bad. Yay, I did it. It probably helps knowing that if you've picked up this book, you either a. know who I am already and got the book to support me, or b. you don't know me at all and regardless of that, you're just interested in the things I offer to talk about. Cool!

If you're in the first group, thanks for supporting me and picking up this book, I super appreciate it! If you're in the second group, THANK YOU with extra sprinkles on top because you were just interested in this book and its topics and I didn't even peer pressure you into buying it to support a friend!

Oh hey, you'll probably notice from that last paragraph that I sometimes fall into this thing called "self-deprecating" humor which is a pretty well known genre of this thing I like to call "humor as a coping mechanism." Oops. It happens.

But Coltan, how can you be talking throughout this book about love and positivity when you're cracking jokes at your own expense and making fun of yourself? Why, let me tell you!

The very first thing I need to let you know, the very first secret to let you in on, is that I'm human. We all are. Here I am, talking to you about self-compassion. Do I sometimes slip up and make mistakes? Absolutely.

It is impossible for any human to be perfect at anything. And as a kid with undiagnosed ADHD, major imposter syndrome, and low self-esteem, believe me, I TRIED.

Artwork: Chia Lor | www.chialor.com

However, this brings me to a point that I think is really important for you to know right from the very beginning with this journey we're embarking on together. Are you ready? The first mic drop, truth bomb, golden nugget, etc. of the book?

Okay... Here goes... You sure you're ready?...

It is profoundly and exponentially more self-compassionate to forgive ourselves for our temporary lapses in self-compassion than to strive for—or even achieve—perfect, consistent, and constant self-compassion.

There are a multitude of similar or parallel ideas in our society that get to this same point. The moral of the story is that how we can experience unlimited good becomes meaningless if we can't also find the grace and kindness to overcome the bad. It's not about us falling, but about the fact that we get back up.

THÈM DE LA CRÈME

If you take absolutely anything away from this book, I want it to be this point: consistency and achievement in your efforts are great, and they should be rewarded. Where the true victories will come in this process is the ability to acknowledge those imperfections with grace and self-love that is unconditional.

This road to unconditional self-love and self-acceptance isn't easy. I've been on that road for years now. And who knows, there probably isn't some magical destination at the end of the road where you finally "get it" 100% of the time. I wouldn't know because, like I said, I haven't gotten to that point and I'm not really sure if anyone ever has. But the fact that you're still taking it is all that matters, because the journey will always be worthwhile in the end, and you are deserving of that journey along with whatever progress and growth you are able to find.

At the beginning of my own journey, I was a young, closeted, pre-transition kid in a very small and very midwestern town. I moved to Menomonie for college in 2013. I recall thinking this small, quaint town was absolutely massive because it had a full department store and more than two fast food restaurants.

While there are millions of experiences I had growing up under those contexts that I wouldn't wish on anyone and I'm sure you can imagine, I also can't say that I regret having them either. They made me who I am.

I was always bullied as a kid. If it wasn't because I was feminine, it was because I was read as queer before I even knew that for myself. If not that, my weight.

Most of the bullying was teasing and verbal harassment. While I was fortunate to find physical violence as a rarity in my bullying experiences, there were also some occurrences of sexual harassment and violence toward me from boys trying to "make an example" of me as a queer boy. I believe the first time I seriously contemplated ending my own life because of the torment was around ten years old.

Don't worry, there's a light at the end of the tunnel of that doom and gloom. When I was twelve, I joined a community theatre for the first time and was heavily involved until shortly before my college years. Outside of family, I'm pretty sure this theatre troupe was one of the first times I truly felt like I understood and had experienced unconditional love and support and I believe this had a profound impact on me.

Being around them was the first time I heard someone's queerness talked about in more than a whisper or the local gossip. Transness was openly welcomed and accepted and embraced and we talked about things like people's correct name and pronouns. Naturally, they were some of the first people that I came out to when I was in high school. To no one's surprise, I was met with unconditional acceptance.

If I could boil it down to a very simple level, I believe that some of these profound experiences of acceptance are some of the exact reasons that many of my life's trajectories have been influenced by a deep need to ensure others feel that same sense of acceptance and love.

In high school, I saw my own experiences as an out queer student and advocated for a student organization where LGBTQIA+ and ally students could gather and feel safe. After briefly studying apparel design, I quickly changed my undergrad major to something for fields like counseling or social work.

Throughout college, I worked at an LGBTQIA+ Resource Center, held leadership roles in student government at the university and statewide levels, published research on transgender discrimination and poverty, and so many other things. As I mentioned previously, part of the through line here is the undiagnosed ADHD and need to be doing all the things, but the other major theme was the desire to help people and advocate for people to feel loved and accepted.

In addition to those things being outlets for my desires of making people feel loved and affirmed, they were also spaces where I began to receive immense amounts of that support and affirmation and love as well.

I wouldn't even be remotely near where I am today if it wasn't for the profound love and support that I've been blessed to receive by so many. The unconditional love and affirmation from all of them just further shows this is something everyone needs.

Photos: Miranda Wipperfurth, MLW Photography | www.mlwphotollc.com

About five years ago, I began transitioning and came out as nonbinary and I took a pretty big hit to my confidence and my feelings of being loved, supported, and seen. I knew that presenting in such a non-conforming way as I do would definitely have some pushback.

Slurs, erasure, disrespect of my pronouns and identity, saying my transition was for "attention," you name it. On some nights, I would even find that I would be walking home past the bars downtown and men would hurl slurs and I'd overhear them debating following me home. Harassment on dating sites was also commonplace for me, which really drove in the question of whether I was even worthy of love at all.

Then, I met Jacob.

Jacob has been a blessing in my life and has been the example of kindness that I needed to reaffirm that I am worthy of love that is completely unconditional.

Meeting the love of my life in tandem with my training as a therapist has truly been the perfect cocktail to revive my passion for a more loving world.

Recipes and baking are a lot like working on ourselves, now that I think about it.

Some steps are more or less work, some processes might need your undivided attention, and others may happen naturally if everything's there.

Our journeys are all going to have different steps and that's okay.

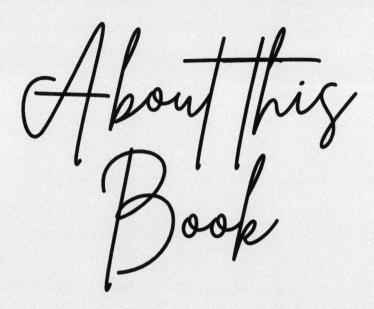

About This Book

Let's talk for a minute about how this whole thing is going to go.

Do you have your frilly pink apron on? Washed your hands? Preheated the oven? Just kidding about the oven. Don't turn on your oven unless you're actually about to bake something because electricity is expensive. Also, fire hazards and stuff? However, if you actually are reading this book with washed hands and a frilly pink apron on, I love it. Keep up that energy.

If you haven't done any of those things, that's okay too. It was more of a rhetorical question to get you excited because we're about to get into it.

As we get ready to dive in, most of the purpose of this section is to get some of the base understandings laid out about the way this book will operate and some things to know and keep in mind as we go on this journey together.

"CHALLENGE BY CHOICE"

All I can think of regarding how to start this part is that internet meme where people just say "we live in a society" with no context. But it's true. We live in a society. With any society, they have a collection of ideas and understandings and ways of operating. The society I live in as I write this book (and perhaps the same society that you live in) is one that has a lot of ideas that are going to be challenged by this book, and that's okay.

The society I'm talking about, particularly the United States and some parts of broader western culture, is a capitalistic society that puts profit and revenue in a higher priority than the wellbeing of its citizens. This is especially true for the indigenous communities who have the true and original claim to the lands we stand upon, as well as the black and brown bodies who have built this country with their bare hands. Even now, they continue to face violence and oppression rather than reaping the benefits of their own exploited labor.

Before I go any further with that point, I need to take a brief aside to relish the fact that I'm discussing such critical issues in a pink cookbook littered with cupcakes and sprinkles and glitter is just absolutely wonderful. The juxtaposition of the serious content and playful visuals is simply marvelous.

Carrying on, a side effect of such a capitalistic and exploitative society is the engrained patterns we have been trained into of constantly devaluing ourselves and fixating on correction of our deficits and finding or making up new deficits to correct when we run out.

Close your eyes and imagine a window. Oh, wait a minute. Full transparency here, I went on for a few more paragraphs and then looked back and realized to myself, "How are they going to keep reading what I tell them if I told them to close their eyes?" Anyways, back to the window. Just picture it in your mind's eye as you're reading this. How many panes does it have? Is there a decorative frame? Maybe it's stained glass. Or maybe there are some cute trinkets adorning the sill. Can you see it? Good. Keep it there in your mind's eye.

Open that window in your mind for me because we're taking those ideas about devaluing ourselves and our deficits and we're going to count to three before THROWING THEM OUT OF THAT WINDOW.

Moral of the story here, this book is going to be challenging a ton of those beliefs that we have inside all of us.

It's important to acknowledge that from the very beginning, because you have a right to consent to this journey, and that's really important to me. Part of that is being transparent with you about your ability to choose how you engage. This book is going to challenge a lot of what we've been told all of our lives.

I think that many of these ideas are harmful to us and create patterns of self-shame and devaluing our own worth and right to love, as well as compromise our abilities to lovingly engage with each other as citizens of this world. That's my opinion. As we challenge many of these beliefs that have led to these patterns, some of them may be incredibly difficult to undo or unlearn. That's okay.

After all of that, here is the one thing I will ask of you: challenge by choice. Both of those words are very important with this request. I ask that you challenge yourself and embrace discomfort as we discuss some of these things. However, your choice is also important in that I don't want anyone engaging in ways that move beyond stretching their capacity and into the territory of just causing them harm. What those limits will look like is different for everyone, and the decision is up to you.

"VARIETY IS THE SPICE OF LIFE"

You know how I just said that everyone's capacities and comfort levels are different for each person? So many things are. That's the beauty of being human.

Comparison is one of those sneaky tricks that we learn early on that is an incredibly efficient way of finding deficits. The grass might be greener on the other side, sure. But, maybe their grass is fake? Or maybe they painted it a greener shade? Or perhaps their soil just naturally is more fertile for grass. What does it matter? Besides, manufactured and manicured lawns are so 1950s. Natural biodiversity and thriving organic gardens are all the rage.

The point that I'm trying to make here is that we all have infinitely different factors in who we are, our backgrounds, our surroundings, our access, and so many other contexts that make no two human experiences identical. You are the sum of all of those contexts and they will absolutely impact a majority of your experiences, including the things you get out of this book.

Enjoy this process, as well as the delicious recipes along the way. Don't tarnish your bliss worrying about what someone else might be gaining or experiencing from these discussions, or wonder if any of the recipes you try look or taste like mine or other people's. In fact, this also brings up a very intentional and deliberate decision that I made when I began working on this book.

You might have noticed by now that this book is a moderately visual one. Okay, it's VERY visual. There's more photos scattered about in this book than the box with all of my childhood pictures growing up that I would spend ages rummaging through trying to find that one specific picture—of which I never found, because why would I?

There's a specific choice that I made in that this book is very visual, just as there was deliberate intention as to what the photos were. I believe that the visual nature of this book not only makes for a more enjoyable reading experience, but also makes the challenging moments we'll have feel less threatening.

Now, for the controversial plot twist: you would think that a cookbook like this would have photos of my work. Influencers or celebrities do that when they have cookbooks out, right? All of those gorgeous photos of their meals, delicately staged for maximum beauty atop immaculate marble counters that cost more than my student loan debt after a Master's Degree? I'm broke, y'all. Granted, I know my way around a camera and could have made it work, sure. However, wouldn't that just make comparison rear its ugly head again?

"So let me make sure I'm hearing you right, Coltan. You don't have pictures of the food you have recipes for in this book?" Yep. Don't get me wrong, I still want to live that influencer cookbook fantasy, visually. Who wouldn't? So on the recipes and throughout the rest of this book, photos are just stock photos I have licenses for that will serve more as a mood setter, rather than an example to follow. These recipes should inspire you, not direct you. If you make one of these recipes and it comes out looking similar to mine, great! I love that. But it's not the goal. I want you to play and have fun with these recipes, and not limit yourself to a goal of matching perfectly.

Recreation, not re-creation.

It would be hypocritical of me to talk about how we all come from different backgrounds and different contexts that influence our experience and have a recipe with a picture of my work slapped on it saying "this is what you should be going for."

All the same, you should not expect me to be talking about any of the other topics that we'll address through this book followed up with a "this is what you should be going for." We're all going to get different things out of our exploration of our relationships with ourselves and others just as much as we all have different things we will have and be able to offer putting into this experience.

"YOU CATCH MORE FLIES WITH HONEY"

I'm sure we've all heard that phrase. Normally, it's in the context of saying that if we're trying to persuade someone to do something, we should be nice about it. I think many of us have likely internalized this phrase and put it into practice with everyone we meet except for the most important person to remember it for: ourselves.

Think about it for a second. How often is it that, when we make a mistake or are trying to grow, we are immensely hard on ourselves. Think about some of the things you say to yourself and ask yourself if you'd ever say that to a friend or loved one. No? Why not? Let me guess. "They don't deserve those words."

Surprise, dear reader: YOU DON'T DESERVE THEM EITHER.

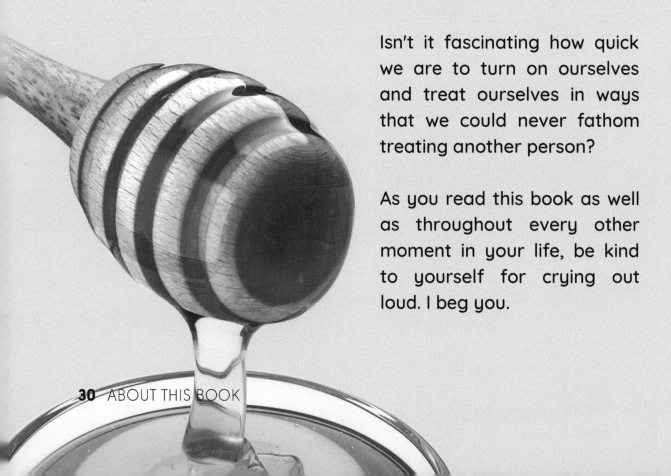

Isn't it fascinating how quick we are to turn on ourselves and treat ourselves in ways that we could never fathom treating another person?

As you read this book as well as throughout every other moment in your life, be kind to yourself for crying out loud. I beg you.

I've said time and time again that this book is going to be challenging a lot of things we have buried deep inside us and may even open up some wounds we didn't even realize were there. That doesn't mean that this can't be a positive and even, dare I say, fun and joyful experience.

If any frame or perspective is the dominant lens through which you read this book, let it be one of kindness. Embrace the process and go forward with the belief that you deserve joy and happiness. Make the deliberate decision that you see your worth and acknowledge your humanity. Give yourself the grace to make mistakes. Be imperfect and messy without those things becoming indicators of inherent flaw or deficit.

I am but one human with a lot of opinions. However, there is one thing I know as an objective, undeniable fact: you are deserving of those kindnesses. I promise.

In addition to kindness, you are deserving of healing from wounds that your life or circumstances have left you with. As you engage with these ideas, I strongly implore you to seek further healing if this work identifies such injury or scars. Be it talking to a close friend, seeking support from a religious or community leader, or even seeking counseling or therapy options that might be available to you. I don't suggest therapy because you are so broken that only a professional could intervene as many would think, but instead because you are deserving of healing and repair in an efficient and supportive manner, no matter how big or small the wound.

Getting something right on the first try is great and all, but there's something special about that moment when you finally nail it after so many attempts.

You let out an exhale of relief that almost feels like you're breathing for the first time.

In a way, you're reborn as a new person, one who was capable of doing it all along.

Baking 101

Some initial hints that might be helpful as we get started, whether you've been baking for five minutes or five decades.

Hooray, you made it! We're actually going to talk about baking now! Thank you for staying with me while we got all that preliminary groundwork taken care of. Your patience will be worth it, I promise.

If you know me personally, you know that I'm a nerd for context and that love for background leads me to have an exasperatingly long build up to make sure that all of the appropriate context to what I'm saying has been given its proper inclusion in the conversation. Especially during the times of pandemic that this book is written, I think my fiancé who has been quarantining with me all this time has been the most severe victim of my long-windedness. Sorry, Jacob.

However, as is the case with any long-winded rant that seems to be going in a million directions, there is a point to this and a method to my madness. Scout's honor. And yes, I was a boy scout. I mean, technically cub scout but still. And the irony is now I'm neither a scout nor a boy. Oops.

Just as when I am in one of my long-winded rants, proper context and build up is essential before we get started. It makes me think of the conversation of equality versus equity. One of my friends used the metaphor one time that equality is everyone getting a pair of shoes and they're all the same size. Some may have shoes already and not need them or be a different size than the ones provided. In an equitable situation, everyone who needs shoes would receive them and it's made sure that they're in the correct size.

In a way, I feel like it's more equitable to be intentional about providing as much context as possible. As I've reiterated thus far, people are coming from various different backgrounds and experiences which provides all of us with varying amounts of information. Additional attention to providing context, in my opinion, is an effort to close that information gap.

Some people reading this have probably baked for decades longer than I've even been on this earth. Other people may even just be reading this book right now and thinking to themself, "Baking sounds fun, maybe I should try it." The spectrum in between the two is vast and infinite. Aside from volume of experience, the source of said experience can vary too. Some of you might have learned your skills during your childhood from your family. Maybe you studied culinary arts from the masters themselves while abroad and you're now known as a major online personality and chef (in which case, you might be Claire Saffitz. Claire, if you're reading this, hi, big fan). Or maybe you're self-taught by reading articles and watching online video tutorials where you're shown the ropes by charismatic people making it look exponentially easier than it probably was thanks to movie magic. Naturally, those quirky but informative hosts may or may not, once again, be Claire Saffitz.

Everyone is coming into this grand adventure we call baking with different skill sets, tools, talents, understanding, and knowledge. If I am to make this book an equitable experience, it's only fair that I pay attention to that fact and ensure that a good foundation layer is set for anyone who might need it.

Some of the information throughout this 101 section may seem really elementary. I'm sure it probably is. But it might not be. I think of "The Star Thrower" by Loren C. Eiseley where the child was throwing starfish back into the ocean. Upon being questioned by others who drew attention to the fact that she couldn't possibly make a difference and save them all. She tosses another in the sea and responds "I made a difference for that one!" Even if many might not need all of the context and explanation while leading into the recipes throughout this book, some people might benefit from it. That makes it all worth it.

So that we're all on the same page, here is some basic Baking 101 that will prove helpful for the recipes in this book and other baking adventures.

Terms, Tips, & Tricks

Baking Powder: A powder that contains sodium bicarbonate (baking soda) and an acid, which activates when exposed to liquid and helps baked goods rise.

Baking Soda: Sodium bicarbonate, a substance that reacts when exposed to a liquid and acid which helps baked goods rise.

Batter: This is the raw combination of ingredients that will be baked into a cake. Batter is more liquid and is poured into its appropriate baking dish, whereas a dough for something like bread or cookies would be more solid and can be hand-worked, kneaded, or cut.

Beat: Rapidly mix together.

Brown Sugar: Available in light or dark variations, brown sugar contains molasses which leads to its color and stickier consistency. Many recipes call for brown sugar to be packed tightly when measuring.

Confectioner's Sugar: Also called powdered sugar, this sugar is ground into a fine powder rather than crystals. Because of its finer, powdery texture, confectioner's sugar mixes with other ingredients more smoothly and is a favorite ingredient for buttercreams and icings or as a light dusting for garnish.

Creaming: With ingredients like butter or cream cheese, creaming is the process of mixing softened ingredients together so that they become one uniform consistency rather than separate units like sticks of butter or blocks of cream cheese.

Cupcake Liners/Papers: These are the individual cups that line the muffin tin to minimize sticking to the pan and limit cleanup as well as provide a wrapper for the cupcakes. Most commonly, liners are paper or other materials and are disposable. However, some liners can be made out of materials like silicone which allow them to be reusable.

Extract: Extracts, like vanilla extract, are traditionally an alcohol or other liquid that is infused with ingredients to flavor it and then concentrated. Extract is used to flavor baked goods. Extracts can be expensive because of the natural flavors and ingredients, so some artificial flavors also offer a more affordable route.

Fold: Gently mix by pulling under the mixture with your spoon or spatula and then fold it over itself, doing so repeatedly until everything is mixed together. Folding is usually required when more rigorous mixing could compromise the texture or consistency of the mixture and a more gentle hand is needed to mix without deflating or otherwise compromising your mixture.

Garnish: This is a decorative element and is usually the finishing touch on a dessert. Examples could include a dusting of powdered sugar, adding fruit and/or whipped cream on top, decorating with nuts or chocolate shavings, or decorating with edible flowers.

Granulated Sugar: Plain, white sugar crystals which dissolve and sweeten recipes. Granulated sugar, as with other sugars, can also melt and caramelize.

Heavy Cream: Also known as heavy whipping cream, this dairy product is used commonly in baking as a thicker and creamier addition to sauces or other recipes compared to milk. When whipped, heavy cream is incorporated with air and becomes stiff, thus whipped cream.

Inserting a Toothpick: This is a test used in baking to ensure that your bake is fully cooked through. If the middle is still raw, a toothpick would have batter on it when you pull it out. A "clean" toothpick does not have batter on it when you remove it because the batter has been baked fully.

Muffin Tin: Also known as a cupcake tin or cupcake pan, this is the specialty cookware that provides individual wells for your cupcakes to sit inside of as they bake. Variations include size of the wells for larger or smaller cupcakes/muffins, as well as the number of wells in any given pan such as a dozen, two dozen, or half dozen.

Peaks: When whipping, peaks are the different indicators of how whipped the consistency is. "Peaks" refers to the small, mountain-like shape that happens when you remove your whisk and some of the whip is pulled upward. "Soft" peaks means a moderate whip. When pulling up your whisk, the peak will hold its shape although the very top will fall in on itself slightly, creating a curling effect. "Stiff" peaks means a sturdier whip. When pulling up your whisk, the peak that is formed will be stiff and almost entirely hold its shape.

Piping: This is a way of applying frosting (or things like mashed potatoes if you want to jazz up your dinner plate) by extruding through a cone-shaped bag, usually made of plastic or other materials, and placed in a pattern in a decorative manner. Special decorative tips are usually applied to the piping bag which create various effects when the frosting exits the tip.

Preheat: This is a basic function of most ovens, which allows the oven to gradually rise to the intended temperature. Most recipes call for you to preheat your oven first so that it heats up while you prepare your batter or dough and the oven is fully heated by the time you are ready to bake.

Whip: This is the motion of rapidly stirring ingredients, such as cream, so that air becomes incorporated into the mix.

Zest: This is tiny shreds of the exterior of a fruit, such as a lemon, lime, or orange. This part of the fruit holds a large amount of the respective fruit's flavor and can be a great way to add flavor without adding extra liquid to a recipe like juices would.

Other Tips That Aren't Glossary Terms

Softening Butter: Naturally, the best way to get softened butter when it's called for in a recipe is to leave it out at room temperature for an hour or two before you get started. Sometimes, schedules don't allow for that or we forget. In a pinch, put the butter in the microwave at the defrost setting for about thirty seconds to a minute or so per stick, depending on your specific microwave. Keep an eye on it though. If it starts melting, pull it out.

Maintaining Oven Temp: If you aren't among the fortunate to have a window on your oven with which to check on your baked goods and have to open your oven to check, be quick about your checking. The longer your oven is open, more hot air escapes and the oven's temperature drops. If you're wanting to do the toothpick check, pull it out quickly and close the oven while you check. Even if the bake cools slightly out of the oven, at least it's going back into a still-hot oven if it needs more time.

Overbaking and Underbaking: This takes some practice but has worked wonders for me. If your bake is just slightly underdone (and I mean very slightly), pull it out anyways. My observations have noted that the best consistency of a baked good comes from pulling them out slightly underdone and letting them bake the very last bit while they're still in the hot pan. Then they're perfectly cooked through and not overbaked and dried out. On the reverse side, if you burn your bake a little, you can always shave off the burnt bits with a grater or zester. Bring back moisture by drizzling some simple syrup (equal parts sugar and water heated up until all the sugar is melted) into the exposed part of your bake so it soaks up the extra moisture and prevents it from going dry.

Buttermilk: If you're in a pinch and don't have buttermilk or can't justify purchasing a whole carton when the recipe calls for so little, you can use a tablespoon of an acid like vinegar or lemon juice and add it to a cup of milk (so adapt that to however much buttermilk you need if it requires a different amount than a cup). Let that sit for a bit and you have buttermilk.

Parchment Paper: If you're baking something more flat like a cake or cookies, parchment paper is your best friend. Similar to how cupcake liners separate the cupcakes from the pan, parchment paper does the same thing. It saves so much time on dishes.

Paint a Picture for 'Em: This is more of some general wisdom rather than actual instruction. When it comes to presentation or deciding how you'll decorate a cupcake (or even a whole cake), there's some considerations to think about. If you are going to be baking where there may be multiple flavors available, intentional decorating can be vital. Even if you're only offering one type of treat, perhaps people may want to avoid certain desserts for dietary, allergy, or preference reasons.

With that being said, a widely accepted understanding is that it is a courtesy to garnish and decorate your cupcakes or cakes in a way that people can easily determine the flavor of your treat. This doesn't necessarily mean that all of your cupcakes need to be garnished with literal neon signs screaming their flavor or nutrition labels printed on edible sugar paper. However, there should be some sense of a through line where one can pick up on the subtle hints in your decorating. With cupcakes, you get a little bit more wiggle room because of seeing some of the exposed cake around the exterior, but a fully frosted cake would especially benefit from this rule. Even then, unless you're doing something like red velvet that you can make out from across the room, the hints are still appreciated.

Chocolate cake with peanut butter filling? Throw a mini peanut butter cup on top. Cookies 'n creme? Use some extra cookie crumbs. Lemon? Sprinkle some lemon zest on top, or (if you're feeling frisky) make some lemon twists to garnish. Carrot cake? Top with candied carrot or little frosting carrot designs.

How to Pipe Your Frosting:

- First, determine your bag and your tip. Using a coupler will have extra steps but allows you to easily swap out different tips. With couplers, insert the primary piece in the trimmed bag, then your tip, then the end piece that locks everything together. If you are not using a coupler, simply insert your tip into the piping bag after trimming the very tip off. If you're unsure about how much to cut off, start small. You can always trim more off for a better fit but won't be able to add more if your piping tip is falling out.

- Once your bag and tip are properly assembled, I use a glass or other container to stand the bag up and fold the very top of the bag inside out over the glass with a generous overhang. When you take the bag back out, this will ensure the top is free of frosting and less messy.

- Fill your piping bag with your frosting of choice. Once it is full, you can pull that lip back up and give the bag a slight shake to move all the frosting toward the bottom and minimize air bubbles. Then, take those nice, clean edges at the top and begin twisting it to close the frosting within the bag. The tighter, the better.

- Holding the bag in one hand, fold that twisted top over and grasp the top of the piping bag with your other hand, pinning the excess bag under your palm and positioning a firm grip over the top of the bag.

- With this grip over the top of the bag, begin to apply firm and consistent pressure. This will push frosting down and out of the bag through the tip, piping frosting wherever you are aiming the tip.

How powerful you must be to take a recipe that would normally do you harm and use wit and creativity to make a reality where that threat of harm is no longer a concern in enjoying it.

How infinitely magical it is to use your mind when posed with the choice of harm or abstinence and choose joy instead.

Substitutions

A multitude of considerations for making any of these recipes, and any others you may find, to accommodate for any dietary needs we and our loved ones might have.

I really think my friend Ryan put it best. When I was working on this book and getting some ideas from people about various ways to navigate the challenges of accommodating various dietary needs when preparing a meal or making a dessert, he dropped this absolute gem on me:

"But, the challenge means that whatever I make is made with love, and I kind of love the idea that cooking with someone's health or dietary restrictions in mind is a love language."

I couldn't have said it better myself, and that's why I'm so thankful for so many amazing, thoughtful, and considerate people like Ryan in my life. And he's right! While it may be extra work or challenge to navigate different dietary needs within a recipe, especially if there's multiple different needs involved, it can absolutely be a way to show that you care and are considerate of those you're cooking or baking for.

With baking, especially something as involved as cupcakes, there's so many different types of considerations you have to make. Gluten, sugar, dairy, eggs, and even possible allergens like nuts or cocoa are all factors that need to be considered.

Having said that, it's important to note that ways to go about dietary restrictions, just like the restrictions themselves, are going to be different for everyone. Some people may think one way to handle a certain allergy or intolerance is great, whereas it may not for someone else who has the same allergy or intolerance as well but also have it for the very thing that would substitute it.

I'm by no means an expert on different ways to substitute for various dietary needs. And really, the only person who will be the best expert for any dietary needs is the person who has them. We are all the best experts of our own experience. However, I do think that it is important to still try and provide some tips and tricks for you all with different ways to navigate some of the common needs that you might encounter in your baking.

For each dietary restriction that I'll talk about, I've recognized that I am —once again—not the expert. With that in mind, I am fortunate to have a great and supportive community of people (like Ryan and others) who've happily shared their amazing tips with me on how to navigate various different dietary needs.

I'm sure that the list of dietary restrictions that I come up with, just as the list of ways to address each one, will definitely not be exhaustive. Please make sure to trust your own body and your own experiences with any sort of ways that you try to navigate these options for accommodating dietary restrictions. I am not a medical provider or a registered dietitian, nor are any of the other people who've been generous enough to provide these nuggets of wisdom. Just as they are my friends and community, think of this section as some friendly advice sharing or swapping some life hacks and each tip may work differently for everyone.

Feel free to enjoy these various tips and tricks and use as needed with any of the recipes in this book, or any other recipes you may come across in your bountiful baking adventures..

Just like Ryan said, these tips can be a way to bake with someone's health and dietary needs in mind and is, in its own way, a form of expressing love. I think that's beautiful.

Also, as I was writing these sections about substitutions I realized that many of these could also serve as replacements for other reasons than dietary. Perhaps, in a momentary lapse of preparation, you got started on a baking project and realized you're out of something, but you don't want to put on real person pants or mascara to leave the house and run to the store, which of course has NEVER happened to me ever... Not once... I don't know what you're talking about...

Being thoughtful about needs around flour or gluten can, in many ways, be one of the most important substitutions. While other types of sensitivities or allergies may result in some unpleasant digestive impacts, a gluten intolerance like celiac disease could have major consequences that we want to avoid.

What can make this all the more difficult is the fact that flour, in many baked goods, is one of the most significant ingredients and usually is the largest quantity in the recipe.

Thankfully, there's a multitude of ways that we can navigate this. As gluten-free diets become more and more common, many brands are looking to provide a solution and so are the grocery stores that stock their products. One of the simplest ways to navigate a flour substitution to avoid gluten is to purchase a specialty flour.

With the wide variety of options, however, leads us to the need of being intentional with our selection. As I mentioned earlier, solutions are not one-size-fits-all. What makes the difference for accommodating one person may bring up all new issues for another person.

Thankfully, I've got a bunch of wonderful friends who've shared their gluten-free tips and tricks with me, and have allowed me to share them with you!

wheat, flour, or gluten

"Rice flour works well for gluten-free food but you have to use a binding agent if making a bread because it will fall apart easily."
-Da'kota M.

"When using gluten-free all-purpose flour, I've found things to be a bit drier than wheat flour so I add just a little bit more liquid to whatever I am making! My favorite gluten free flour is Pillsbury™ brand" -Megan R.

"When I bake and use gluten free flour, my biggest takeaway is oil and applesauce instead of butter. It tends to make it stay together and hold better flavor!" -Ellie M.

"Namaste® Perfect Flour Blend is my favorite for baking as I think it has the most similar texture and no difference in taste to regular baked goods, other than being a little denser." -Meghan H.

"My wife is allergic to dairy, rice, gluten, and oats. This makes baking tricky as most GF flours include rice flour. We opt for Bob's Red Mill® All Purpose GF Flour (in the red bag) for most of our baked goods. I also have found that a 75/25 ratio of GF flour/almond flour makes our baked goods more fluffy and moist. GF flour tends to be dry and the almond flour retains moisture really well in my experience." -Courtney B

"I have hypoglycemia, so I really appreciate substitutions... any time almond flour can be used in combination with or instead of white flour, it makes my body happy."
-Rickie Ann L.

Just like our friends flour and gluten, milk and dairy products can also be complicated to substitute. While milk and dairy aren't usually as prominent players in a recipe like flour would be, dairy's complication comes from the large number of forms it may appear as in any given recipe, possibly even multiple times!

Baking recipes could call for so many types of dairy. There's milk (plus the debacle of some recipes specifying a certain level of fat content like whole milk vs. 2% vs. skim), heavy whipping cream, sour cream, cream cheese, mascarpone, yogurt, and goodness knows what else! Also, apologies to any of my lactose-intolerant friends or readers who felt impending doom of gas or indigestion just from reading that list.

You'll also note I didn't even mention butter, which is possibly the most prominent dairy in baking. Don't worry, we'll get there. Since butter is used more as a source of fat in baking which differs from what the other types of dairy are used for, butter has its own page.

Replacing dairy in your baking is one of the more easily accessible ways to alter a recipe. With the prevalence of lactose-intolerance and growing popularity of

milk and other dairy

vegan diets, many dairy alternatives are available. In most cases, finding a direct substitute will be the solution. For example, does a recipe need milk? Use almond, soy, or coconut milk, depending on your personal taste and which flavor may pair best with your intended treat. Same with cream cheese or yogurt. Plenty of these products will have dairy-free options. For other tips, let's ask my friends again!

"Coconut milk + lemon juice = sour cream substitute. Silken tofu + lemon juice is a good substitute for yogurt. Mix first before adding. It'll separate if it sits too long, so you just have to re-emulsify if separation occurs." -Chelsea R.

"Unsweetened almond milk always works fine in place of milk for me. I have used canned coconut milk in place of buttermilk in coffee cake and again, it turned out just fine." -Mellie A.

"Almond milk replaces dairy milk and voila, I can follow almost any recipe without too much headache!" -Courtney B.

"I use plain, unsweetened almond milk (or vanilla almond milk if you want a little vanilla flavor) and that always seems to work well in place of milk, cream, etc." -Meghan H.

"I am lactose intolerant and pescatarian, so lots of switching and vegan recipes happen naturally. For recipes that require ricotta, I just blend up some tofu... Also coconut milk is a dream come true when replacing heavy cream in a recipe." -Kylie A.

"Lactose-free cream cheese from Whole Foods® is incredible." -Meghan L.

"Sub in coconut milk or coconut cream for sauce recipes asking for whipped cream or milk." -Emily B. D.

They wouldn't be called sweets if they didn't taste that way! And that sweet flavor comes from the sugar in a recipe. However, cutting down on sugar or eliminating sugar intake entirely can be a common reason for needing to think creatively about your recipes. As we've seen with the cute little packets that come with our coffee, we are fortunate to have artificial sweeteners at our disposal to maintain that sweet flavor but cut down on the sugar.

For replacing traditional granulated sugar in a recipe, you can opt for natural substitutions for sweet flavors with fruits or syrup, or get containers of artificial sweetener rather easily. This is also the case for other types of sugar like brown sugar or even confectioner's sugar. While those types of replacements are less common, you should still be able to find them in most grocery stores. With confectioner's sugar especially, you should seek out an artificial sweetener version if it is for a recipe where that will be the bulk of the volume, such as a buttercream or icing. However, when confectioner's sugar would be a small part of the recipe or just used for a garnish at the end, you can cheat in a pinch by taking regular artificial sweetener in the same volume that the recipe requires and add one teaspoon of cornstarch for every cup of sweetener before blending at high speed in a food processor until it's a fine powder the same consistency confectioner's sugar would be.

sugar

butter

See? I told y'all we would get to butter. This sassy minx of a dairy product brings flavor to your treats as well as the "cream" in buttercream (but also the "butter," too). For our vegan and lactose-intolerant pals, your options are really straightforward and simple.

Margarine as a vegetable-based alternative to butter is already a great start. But, as MANY of my friends have pointed out and I've also experienced the magic of firsthand, vegan butter is another great route.

If you're specifically lactose-intolerant but aren't vegan or concerned about animal products, ghee is a clarified butter that is lactose free, which I learned from my friends Mellie and Liz.

My friend Mellie also pointed out, "I have also used coconut oil in cake recipes, brownies, etc, and it turns out fine."

Depending on the recipe, if the butter is being used solely as a source of fat, you can also easily replace with another fat like oil.

There's a pun about yolks here that's waiting to happen. I can feel it. In the meantime, the eggs in a recipe serve as a "binder," or the glue that keeps the batter together as it bakes. Just how eggs solidify when you cook them, the same thing kind of happens when you bake eggs in a baked good. The glue sets and it keeps everything together.

As with many of the other ingredients I've said, egg substitutes are available in stores for use in baking. Many of them are in powder form, with instructions for adding different amounts of liquid to emulate egg whites, whole egg, or yolks. It's really cool. First seeing it, I said, "you must be yolking!" (There's the pun, bad I know, but it's better than poaching one off the internet) *ba dum tss*

But, many other alternatives also exist for replacing eggs in your recipe. One trick that I first learned from my mom but has been confirmed further by many of my friends is to use applesauce instead of eggs. Applesauce can also replace butter or eggs in a pinch too. But, as my friend Kai points out, if a recipe has oil, butter, AND eggs, applesauce would not necessarily be a good replacement for all three.

If apples are a no-go due to any allergies or if they conflict with the flavor you're going for, my friends Zen and Liz mention that you can also use bananas, with one banana for each egg. The other alternative my friends Sam, Anne, and Jarrod told me about is a tablespoon of ground flaxseed mixed with three tablespoons of water for each egg.

other substitution tips and tricks

I love all my friends so much. What great humans, and such awesome tips that I really feel have added to the value of this book. I'm so thankful for all of those kind and thoughtful people and I hope that you can think of ways to show appreciation to all of your friends that enrich your life too.

Here were a couple other cool tips and tricks that I thought were amazing but didn't find into any of the other sections very cleanly. Enjoy!

"If you think something needs more salt, but don't want to add more sodium to a dish, try adding something acidic such as lemon or lime juice to your dish. Often times, it's that last bit of flavor you're looking for." -Karlyn D.

"When I get a sweet craving but don't want dairy, I've made sweet potato, cinnamon, soy/almond milk, honey or syrup, and mix it into a paste. Put it in the freezer, it's a great ice cream substitute!" -Ashley S.

"I use ground cashews & nutritional yeast in place of cheese often. Especially for this amazing queso recipe." -Kayla S.

"There are actually a lot of folks who are allergic to corn. an alternative to cornstarch would be tapioca starch." -Mary M.

Part One
LOVING YOURSELF

It's a common trope across media. RuPaul is notorious for his saying, "If you can't love yourself, how in the hell are you gonna love someone else?" Stephen Chbosky writes in my favorite book of my high school years, *The Perks of Being a Wallflower*, "we accept the love we think we deserve." The point: how can we expect to have loving relationships with others if we don't love ourselves?

My critique of these phrases and this idea is that they get warped into something that further isolates people who may already be hurting and doesn't do us any good. It doesn't matter how much or little you love yourself (I mean, it does. That's the point of this part of the book, but you get what I'm saying), you are deserving of love regardless of where you are at with your own self-love journey.

A phrase that I think is significantly more helpful in these cases is that you "can't pour from an empty cup." Our relationships with others are mutual experiences and go both ways. Taking care of ourselves is the most effective way that we can intentionally try to show up as our best selves in that relationship. Part of that care, as I'm sure you've guessed by now, is giving attention to our relationships with ourselves as well.

Just as we deserve to be loved by others, we deserve to love ourselves. A love without condition or exception.

Throughout Part One, we're going to start with that foundation of self-love and compassion, as well as enjoy some fun recipes along the way that are both on the easier end of the spectrum as well as meaningful to me as I think about self-love.

Having areas to grow doesn't make us inferior or less than.

In fact, I think the notion that we can see these areas and work on them is more indicative of our character than any flaw in the first place.

Throw Out That Shame, It's Expired!

Shame has its purposes, but you can always have too much of a good thing.

Oh shame, I know thee well. I don't know your experience, but I know for me that shame has the power to make me feel absolutely sick to my stomach without warning or hesitation. But as I mentioned, there are ways that shame serves us as well. There are plenty of things that can serve us or fulfill our needs, but also can cause pain in the wrong contexts.

Think about this: humans need food and nourishment to survive, right? Regarding nourishment, I can think of all the commercials growing up where they would tell us that we needed to drink milk to be healthy and get calcium that will make our bones stronger. So okay, we need milk to be healthy and thrive (or at least the nutrition associated with it for our vegan or lactose intolerant friends). Here's this thing we NEED, but have any of you had spoiled milk and gotten sick? Food is at the very base level of the hierarchy of needs and we can't live without it, and yet things like food poisoning exist.

Shame also serves a purpose for basic human needs. Humans are social creatures and have depended upon community efforts for survival for all of recorded history. Shame protects us by creating feelings of unease and discomfort around qualities that our brains perceive as threatening to our social survival.

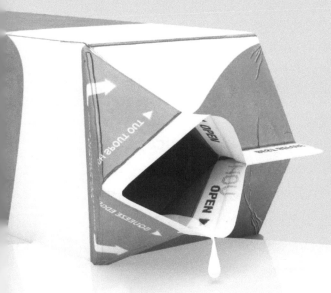

A child may spill milk and begin crying. We say, "don't cry over spilled milk," because we think it's not a big deal. For that child, it's not the milk. Instead, it's the fear of an upset caregiver who may be angry about the mess, and the possibility of rejection for this infraction.

Shame festers within the child in order to say, "Hey, grown-ups might get upset with you if you spill milk. That feels really bad when they're upset so remember this feeling and be more careful next time."

Shame is instinctual and helps us avoid the social faux pas that can theoretically lead to our rejection from communities that help us survive. Shame is working to protect us.

Having said that, is shame very good at its job? Not terribly.

For many of us, shame has spent a majority of our lives working in overdrive. There are plenty of reasons that this could be the case, like certain experiences in our childhood, messaging and attitudes in various cultures and subcultures, and that competitive attitude in society that we need to be better that I've mentioned earlier. Regardless of where it comes from, this experience of having your instincts toward shame being maxed out has profound impacts on our lives.

Think of some of the things you are or have ever felt ashamed about. Through my therapist training, I've firmly held the belief that I shouldn't ask you to do something that I'm unwilling to do myself, so here are some things I've been ashamed of in my life: my weight throughout high school and college, feeling like I cry too much, my less-than-responsible financial skills, being asked to resign from a job because of my mental health at the time, and getting into my Master's Program as an alternate and on academic probation.

Think back to earlier when we discussed some of the things we say to ourselves and whether or not we would also say those things to a friend. With these shames we've listed, responses to the shame can work in the same way.

In some of those shames that I've shared, and likely with some of yours too, there are pretty reasonable responses we can have with them. Okay, you're not great with money? It makes sense that you'd want to strive for better spending and saving habits. I would feel comfortable saying that to a friend and to myself as well. Where the problem ensues is when a small and reasonable amount of shame breeds larger, deeper, and more intrinsic shames. What if, instead of the first response to that shame, my response was something like, "Yeah, you really are horrible with money. Why can't you just grow up and get your act together, it's not that hard. How on earth do you expect to support yourself and not depend on people bailing you out all the time?"

Would you say that to a friend when they express shame about their money habits? No? Me neither. I know for a fact that I've told myself that on MANY occasions. Think about some of the responses you've had to your own shames. I'm sure there's times where you've treated yourself with the same unkindness.

This is how shame, an instinct that has very important purposes as a protection for us social creatures, warps and causes harm. Just like how milk can spoil and make us sick.

When you find yourself feeling shame or self-judgement in the future, think about these things. Is the shame you're feeling telling you something that's a reasonable response to what you're feeling shame about? With what your brain is telling you, would you say the same thing to a friend or loved one? If you're finding these messages aren't a reasonable response and you wouldn't say that to someone in a million years, it's pretty likely that the shame you're experiencing has spoiled. It's gone bad and decayed beyond what would be helpful and hurts you instead. Just like expired milk, it's time to throw it out.

It's important to note, however, that disposing of expired milk isn't done with launching a full container into the recycling with full force. You slowly and carefully let out the milk down the drain. This disposes of the milk properly and doesn't let it splatter about, which would leave you with a smelly mess that's no better than where you started.

Shame works the same way. When we need to dispose of spoiled shame, we do so with a gentle hand. That shame is still a part of us, and does us no good when we alleviate that shame by shaming it right back. Thank that shame for trying its best to be helpful, and let it know that you can take it from here.

CUPCAKE RECIPES
The Basics

Vanilla

A LIGHT AND FLUFFY CLASSIC

This recipe is a great place to start. Delicate and delicious, as well as incredibly versatile. Experiment with different frostings, fillings, and more! Even a beginner will surprise themself with what they're able to create out of this easy and fun recipe!

Ingredients

- 1 1/2 cups all-purpose flour
- 1 1/2 tsp. baking powder
- 1/4 tsp. salt

- 2 large eggs, room temperature
- 2/3 cups granulated sugar
- 1 1/2 sticks (12 tbsp.) melted butter
- 2 tsp. pure vanilla extract
- 1/2 cup milk

Instructions

- Preheat oven to 350°F and fill your cupcake tin with desired cupcake papers or liners.
- Sift flour, baking powder, and salt into a medium bowl before whisking until combined.
- In another bowl, beat eggs and sugar together, gradually adding butter and vanilla. Beat until foamy and light.
- Add half of dry ingredients, then milk, then the remaining dry ingredients, mixing in between. Pour mixture into baking cups to about 3/4 full.
- Bake for 18-20 minutes until an inserted toothpick comes out clean. Allow to fully cool. Customize with fillings, frostings, and garnishes of your choosing.

Makes approximately one dozen cupcakes

We all gotta start somewhere...

I'm afraid of heights, personally. The scariest part of a dive is when you're mustering up the initial courage to jump. Even if you don't reach a destination, every journey you've taken is a time you've seen the heights and jumped anyway. I'm proud of you for that.

Chocolate

TRIED AND TRUE DECADENCE

The dark side of the classic flavor debate, but just as sweet. Similar to vanilla, these chocolate cupcakes are incredibly versatile and pair greatly with a variety of frostings, fillings, and garnishes. For a vegan alternative, check out the bonus recipe "Cocoa Wacky Cake" on pg. 191!

Ingredients

- 3/4 cup all-purpose flour
- 1/2 cup unsweetened cocoa powder
- 3/4 tsp. baking powder
- 1/2 tsp. baking soda
- 1/4 tsp. salt
- 2 large eggs, room temperature
- 1/2 cup granulated sugar
- 1/2 cup packed brown sugar
- 1/3 cup vegetable oil
- 2 tsp. pure vanilla extract
- 1/2 tsp. espresso powder
- 1/2 cup buttermilk

Instructions

- Preheat oven to 350°F and fill your cupcake tin with desired cupcake papers or liners.
- Sift flour, cocoa, baking powder, baking soda, salt, and espresso powder into a medium bowl before whisking until combined.
- In another bowl, mix eggs, sugars, oil, and vanilla together.
- Add half of dry ingredients, then buttermilk, then the remaining dry ingredients, mixing in between. Pour mixture into baking cups to about 3/4 full.
- Bake for 18-21 minutes until an inserted toothpick comes out clean. Allow to fully cool. Customize with fillings, frostings, and garnishes of your choosing.

Don't "Yuck" My "Yum"...

We may bicker about things like chocolate vs. vanilla. But it's okay to like what you like, especially if it's not hurting anyone. You deserve to fully enjoy what gives you bliss, and the same for others. Let this be the end of "guilty" pleasures!

Makes approximately one dozen cupcakes

Red Velvet

IT'LL ROPE YOU IN

A festive, colorful treat. It's often associated with things like Valentine's Day and is also one of my favorites, but I may also be biased because my birthday is Valentine's Day as well.

Ingredients

- 2 1/2 cups all-purpose flour
- 1 1/2 cups granulated sugar
- 1 tsp. baking soda
- 1 tsp. salt
- 1 tsp. cocoa powder
- 1 1/2 cups vegetable oil
- 1 cup buttermilk, room temperature
- 2 large eggs, room temperature
- 2 tbsp. food gel coloring, usually red but other colors can switch it up
- 1 tsp. distilled white vinegar
- 1 tsp. pure vanilla extract

Instructions

- Preheat oven to 350°F and fill your cupcake tin with desired cupcake papers or liners.
- Sift flour, baking soda, salt, and cocoa into a medium bowl before whisking until combined.
- In another bowl, mix eggs, sugar, oil, buttermilk, food coloring, distilled vinegar, and vanilla together.
- Sift dry ingredient mixture into wet mixture and mix until smooth. Pour mixture into baking cups to about 3/4 full.
- Bake for 25-30 minutes until an inserted toothpick comes out clean. Allow to fully cool. You can top with cream cheese frosting and nuts or crumbs, or whatever you choose. My favorite trick is filling with cheesecake!

Makes approximately 12-16 cupcakes

Someone got you seeing red?...

Anger is a fascinating emotion. It often acts as a surface emotion for other feelings like sadness, pain, betrayal, etc. You're allowed to be angry, but allow yourself those other emotions too.

Carrot Cake

SUGAR AND SPICE

Time to switch things up. Carrot cake is one of the more eccentric flavor offerings in this section. Between the use of an unconventional dessert ingredient like carrots and inviting spices to the party, you're in for a satisfying way to spice up your cupcake offerings!

Ingredients

- Optional 1 cup chopped pecans
- 1 1/2 cups packed brown sugar
- 1/2 cup granulated sugar
- 1 cup vegetable oil
- 4 large eggs
- 3/4 cup unsweetened applesauce
- 1 tsp. pure vanilla extract
- 2 1/2 cups all-purpose flour
- 2 tsp. baking powder
- 1 tsp. baking soda
- 1/2 tsp. salt
- 1 1/2 tsp. ground cinnamon
- 1/2 tsp. ground nutmeg
- 1/4 tsp. ground cloves
- 2 cups carrots, grated or finely chopped in a food processor

Instructions

- Toast pecans according to preference if using them for this recipe.
- Preheat oven to 350°F and fill your cupcake tin with desired cupcake papers or liners. Shred carrots to preferred size.
- Mix together sugars, oil, eggs, applesauce, and vanilla until no lumps remain. In another bowl, sift flour, baking powder, baking soda, salt, cinnamon, nutmeg and clove before combining together.
- Add flour and spice mixture to the wet ingredients, mixing well. Fold in carrots (and toasted, chopped pecans if using them). Pour mixture into baking cups to about 3/4 full.
- Bake for 20-22 minutes until an inserted toothpick comes out clean. Allow to fully cool. Top with cream cheese frosting or other choice of frosting and garnish as you like.

Makes approximately one dozen cupcakes

Carrot Cake Controversy...

Not everyone likes carrot cake. I won't even lie to you, it's not usually at the top of my list. But plenty of people say it's their absolute favorite. There's always people out there who appreciate you and see your value, even if you don't see them.

Cookies 'n' Creme

A FLAVOR POWER COUPLE

Cookies. THOSE cookies. I honestly don't remember a time where I've grabbed a pack of them, a glass of milk, and didn't instantly feel joy. They make everything better, including ice cream. And, of course, cupcakes.

Ingredients

- 6 tbsp. softened butter
- 2/3 cup vegetable oil
- 2 cups sugar
- 1 tbsp. clear vanilla extract (pure vanilla extract is okay)
- 2 2/3 cups all-purpose flour
- 1 tbsp. baking powder
- 1 tsp. salt
- 1 cup milk, room temperature
- 6 large egg whites
- 1-2 cups crushed chocolate sandwich cookies

Instructions

- Preheat oven to 350°F and fill your cupcake tin with desired cupcake papers or liners.
- Cream butter before adding sugar and oil, mixing until smooth. Stir in vanilla.
- Sift flour, baking powder, and salt into another bowl and whisk thoroughly.
- Add half of the dry mixture to the wet mixture and combine. Repeat with milk and then the remaining dry mixture.
- In another bowl, whip or beat egg whites until stiff peaks form. Fold egg whites and crushed cookies into batter. Pour batter into baking cups until 3/4 full.
- Bake for 25-35 minutes until an inserted toothpick comes out clean. Allow to fully cool. Top with your choice of frosting and garnish.

Makes approximately 12-16 cupcakes

When life made you a tough cookie...

Your strength has gotten you through so many things. We can also acknowledge that in those moments you deserved happiness, safety, or peace when life decided you needed to be strong instead.

Pupcakes

A NEW KIND OF PUPPY CHOW

We love our furry friends. The value that a four (give or take) legged companion can provide in the lives of many people is beyond measure. This whole book is about cupcakes and relationships with ourselves and loved ones. We always can find a reason to reward our canine comrades, so do you think I'd honestly leave out including a recipe for them? Much thanks to my friend Zen for this easy recipe!

Ingredients

- 2 eggs
- 1/2 cup peanut butter
  - Make sure the peanut butter doesn't contain Xylitol, which is toxic for dogs.
- 1 tbsp. whole wheat flour
  - For dogs with gluten intolerance or if you don't have whole wheat flour, just use slightly less peanut butter and skip flour
- 1 apple, finely chopped
- 1 tsp baking powder

Instructions

- Preheat oven to 350°F and fill your cupcake tin with desired cupcake papers or liners.
- Combine all ingredients well and fill cups halfway full with your batter.
- Bake for 20 minutes until an inserted toothpick comes out clean. Allow to fully cool. Optionally frost with extra peanut butter.

Makes approximately twelve pupcakes

Never doubt a good pupper...

If you find yourself feeling like no one loves you or cares about you, think of all the dogs you've ever met who loved you without hesitation. Would you doubt them?

Frosting!

WHEN IT ALL COMES TOGETHER

The icing on the cake, literally! For these simple but delicious frostings, you're in luck! They all are virtually the same process, but with slightly different ingredients for their respective flavors.

Instructions

- Cream softened butter (and cream cheese, if applicable) in a stand mixer or with a hand mixer until smooth.
- Slowly add confectioner's sugar in manageable increments, mixing well before adding more. If making chocolate buttercream, add cocoa to the first portion of confectioner's sugar when you mix it.
- As you add more confectioner's sugar, make sure to keep a close eye as you get closer to your desired consistency. When you are close to your consistency, add in your vanilla, and salt.
- If your frosting becomes too thick, you can thin it out with small amounts of milk or heavy cream.
- When the desired consistency is achieved, fill your piping bag or store frosting in an airtight container in the fridge. When using frosting you've made ahead, give a good stir by hand or in your mixer to get it back to a desired consistency as it may have dried slightly.
- If you are coloring your frosting, gel food color is best as it won't affect the liquid content as much. Additionally, go slow. You can always add more color but it's significantly harder to reverse the color you've added.

When you're stirring in the night...

It's okay if you find yourself worrying or anxious about something. Just remember to give yourself the space to recognize when things outside of your control aren't entitled to giving you undue worry or stress.

Vanilla Buttercream

- 1 cup softened butter
- 4 cups* confectioner's sugar
- 3 tbsp.* heavy cream or milk
- 2 tsp.* pure vanilla extract
- 1/4 tsp.* salt

Bonus tip: the vanilla buttercream recipe is a great base for experimenting with other flavors. Try out different extracts or add in different things like peanut butter, caramel, syrups, or a fruit jam!

Chocolate Buttercream

- 1 cup softened butter
- 3 1/2 cups* confectioner's sugar
- 1/2 cup* cocoa powder
- 3 tbsp.* heavy cream or milk
- 2 tsp.* pure vanilla extract
- 1/4 tsp.* salt

Cream Cheese Frosting

- 1/2 cup softened butter
- 8 oz. softened cream cheese
- 3 cups* confectioner's sugar
- 3 tbsp.* heavy cream or milk
- 1 tsp.* pure vanilla extract
- 1/4 tsp.* salt

*These measurements are flexible and may need more or less for taste and consistency

I think it's vital that we give ourselves more credit.

We spend way too much time cross-examining whether the joys in our life were deserved or supposed to happen rather than just enjoy our hard work and patience coming to fruition.

Imitation Vanilla is the Imposter, Not You.

You can fake it 'til you make it, but you're not faking once you've finally made it there.

Have I mentioned yet that I think we're unreasonably hard on ourselves? I did? Okay good. Just making sure. One such way that we're incredibly hard on ourselves is this phenomenon known as "imposter syndrome," which was first known as "the imposter phenomenon" when it was initially introduced in an article by researchers Dr. Pauline R. Clance and Dr. Suzanne A. Imes in the 1970s when they studied this experience.

Originally, the imposter phenomenon was initially discovered and coined in their study of this experience among high-achieving women. However, further research a few years later showed that this was an all-too-common experience that transcended gender and was experienced by nearly everyone.

Think of it this way. You're whipping up a dessert. For this instance, let's say it's some vanilla cupcakes and some vanilla buttercream on top. Maybe you're making them for a work party, or a family get-together, or your child is bringing a birthday treat to school. As you're making them, you suddenly realize that you are freshly out of your pure vanilla extract and have to go with your emergency stock of imitation vanilla hidden away in your pantry because there's no time to run to the store. An even more dramatic instance would be using this imitation vanilla in an emergency when you're revered around town for your recipes using real vanilla straight from the bean.

Say you take these cupcakes to their final destination. Everyone is absolutely obsessed with these cupcakes. Someone even sobs from how good they are. As you receive all of your accolades and praise, all you can think of in your head is the thought that you don't deserve any of this praise because you didn't even use "real" vanilla in your recipe. Why should you be complimented on your cupcakes when you're such a fraud?

This, in essence (pun intended), is how imposter syndrome works. We find ourselves thinking that we've somehow fooled everyone and do not deserve the praise or reward coming our way.

One of the most common ways that this manifests is in the workplace or other contexts where we've had to work hard to find ourselves in that position. Our own self-judgement tells us that we've somehow fooled those who hired us or accepted us and we're not even qualified to be in that position. As I mentioned earlier when we talked about shame, I was an alternate and not originally accepted into my graduate program and started on academic probation. These shames were constantly playing in my head and making me feel like I had fooled the professors into letting me in. I had major imposter syndrome for a large portion of my time in graduate school, and many of my cohort members commonly expressed that they felt the same.

The problem here is that we're underestimating our own skills and qualifications significantly more than any hiring or admissions committee could ever possibly overestimate. Unless you literally had plagiarized your résumé from someone with tenfold more experience than you do, I don't think you're unqualified if you ended up getting it.

Source: Clance, P. R., & Imes, S. A. (1978). The imposter phenomenon in high achieving women: Dynamics and therapeutic intervention. Psychotherapy: Theory, Research & Practice, 15(3), 241–247.
https://doi.org/10.1037/h0086006

Imposter syndrome robs us of our ability to thoroughly enjoy our hard work and patience paying off or our dreams becoming a reality. It deprives us of the well-deserved pride and feelings of accomplishment we should have with those moments.

Let's go back to those vanilla cupcakes. In many situations of imposter syndrome, the lack of qualification or feelings of having fooled people is often unfounded and exaggerated by our own self-criticism. In the vanilla cupcake scenario, there is a tangible reason to suggest the praise is undeserved—the imitation vanilla. I'm a firm believer that, just like those feelings of being unqualified, the compare and contrast of imitation vanilla versus pure vanilla extract versus straight from the bean is highly exaggerated in most cases. For sake of argument though, let's roll with it. Even if imitation vanilla was used for these cupcakes, who cares? The accolades and praise mean that one of two things is happening. A. imitation vanilla doesn't make much of a difference and you made some delicious cupcakes. B. imitation vanilla makes a big difference and you somehow managed to have delicious cupcakes anyways.

In either of those two outcomes, you still made delicious cupcakes, so who cares if you didn't use "real" vanilla? And instead of enjoying the praise, you tell yourself that you don't deserve it and rob yourself of that joy and subject yourself to negative internal messages about your talent.

Where imposter syndrome gets worse is this: just like shame, these messages we tell ourselves have a sneaky way of setting in and becoming deeply buried within our self-image and warping into something profoundly harmful. The occasional self-jab out of modesty is one thing, like joking about how you didn't even use real vanilla for those cupcakes so you're surprised they turned out so well. The larger instances, however, begin to twist stories in our mind that tarnish even our most intrinsic senses of worth.

With my time in graduate school studying marriage and family therapy, the passing thoughts of confusion at how I was picked for a cohort of just over a dozen out of hundreds of applicants quickly warped into thoughts that were determined to rob me of my joy in getting in and being in this field at all. Eventually, the thoughts would remind me about all of the people who were probably more qualified and whose places I had stolen. It even got to the point where I questioned that I could even be a competent and qualified therapist at all.

You deserve the progress you've made in your life, the dreams you've made come true, and all of the praises you get from those who love you and admire you. Don't let yourself believe anything different. Even if the journey isn't perfect or conventional, you did it. Sometimes you need to use imitation vanilla, and I'm sure it still tastes great.

Rainbow Confetti

A DELICIOUS PRIDE TREAT

This cupcake is a fun, colorful, and delicious way to celebrate any occasion. With its vibrant rainbow coloring, one such occasion is Pride. Starting out of civil rights movements led largely by transgender women of color like Marsha P. Johnson & Sylvia Rivera, pride is a celebration of who we are as queer and transgender people. I came out as bisexual/pansexual in 2010, and then came out as nonbinary and began my transition in 2015. This cupcake is a love letter to queer, transgender, nonbinary, and intersex people who show us every day how beautiful and diverse the human experience really is.

Ingredients

CAKE

- 1 and 2/3 cups all-purpose flour
- 1/2 tsp. baking powder
- 1/4 tsp. baking soda
- 1/2 tsp. salt
- 1/2 cup unsalted butter, melted
- 3/4 cup granulated sugar
- 1/4 cup packed light brown sugar
- 1 large egg
- 1/4 cup yogurt, plain or vanilla
- 3/4 cup milk
- 1 tbsp. pure vanilla extract
- 2/3 cup rainbow sprinkles (or other color scheme of your choosing. Do not use nonpareils)

FROSTING

- 1 cup butter, softened
- 4-6 cups confectioner's sugar, more or less for desired consistency
- Milk or heavy cream to thin if needed or desired
- 1-2 tsp. vanilla and pinch of salt for flavor as desired
- Desired colors of gel food color

Being yourself is your journey...

Coming out is an incredibly personal decision for someone to make. If you're out and proud, congratulations for making such a brave decision. If not, don't worry. This is your process and no one should take that away from you.

Instructions

- Preheat oven to 350°F and fill your cupcake tin with desired cupcake papers or liners.
- For the cake, sift and mix flour, baking powder, baking soda, and salt.
- Melt butter in the microwave or on the stove before mixing in sugars by whisking until brown sugar lumps have dissolved and a gritty mixture is created.
- Add in egg, yogurt, milk, and vanilla extract and thoroughly mix.
- Slowly incorporate flour mixture in manageable increments until a thick batter is achieved.
- Slowly fold in sprinkles. Be gentle and only fold until the sprinkles are just combined. Overmixing could make the colors run.
- Pour batter into baking cups until each is about 3/4 full. Bake for approximately 35 minutes or until an inserted toothpick comes out clean. Cool before frosting.
- To make frosting, cream the butter until smooth before gradually adding confectioner's sugar until the desired consistency is achieved. Add heavy cream or milk to thin as needed, and flavor with pure vanilla extract and salt as desired.
- To create the rainbow frosting effect, separate frosting into even portions, one for each color you would like to make. Using gel food coloring, dye each of the separate frosting portions into a different color that you want in your rainbow effect. Go slowly as it is easier to add more color than remove too much.
- When all colors of frosting are made, lay out a sheet of plastic wrap on a clean surface and lay each color of frosting in a thin line next to each other. Roll the plastic wrap into one thick log of rainbow frosting, cut any plastic wrap obstructing the end, and insert into a piping bag with your tip of choice. Some frosting may need to be piped out before decorating in order to get all colors showing through.

Makes approximately one dozen cupcakes.

Cake recipe adapted from Sally's Baking Addiction | www.sallysbakingaddiction.com

Language is a fascinating thing, and there can be profound power in finding the words to describe our experiences. But know that no word will ever hold the power to define your value or worth.

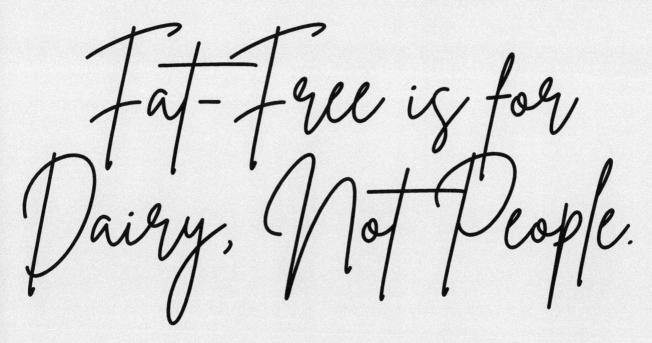

Fat-Free is for Dairy, Not People.

With Special Contribution by Maria Cauley, MS

Like the print on dairy nutrition labels, solely basing our worth on our size or fat content is pretty black-and-white, and as cold as the jar they're printed on.

It isn't lost on me that many would find a cupcake cookbook and a book about healthier ways of living would be mutually exclusive terms. Sure, I get it. But let's break that down a bit.

First and foremost, we need to acknowledge the idea of health is incredibly multifaceted and doesn't look the same from person to person. What might be healthy for one person may not be for another, and something that benefits an aspect of someone's health may do so at the expense of one of the other components of their wellbeing.

The dissonance between a cupcake cookbook and health is based on some ill-informed societal notions. Obviously, I probably wouldn't advise any individual person making one of the recipes in this book to eat all twelve of their beautiful cupcakes by themselves and in one sitting. I firmly believe that sharing is caring, first of all. Secondly, most experts would probably not find a lot of nutritional value in such a thing. However, you gotta do what you gotta do at the end of the day and if twelve cupcakes is what you need, I won't shame you for it. So putting that point aside, the notion of a cupcake cookbook and information about health being mutually exclusive continues to do a massive disservice to the very idea of what health is in the first place.

The very first place many of us go when we think of health is food and our bodies. However, there are so many more aspects to our health and wellbeing than the most literal and physical perspectives of the conversation. Like I mentioned before, some "health efforts" could be profoundly damaging to other aspects of our wellbeing, so why do we pigeonhole health into such a small and unrealistic box?

We are more than a number.

As humans, we are more complex than we could ever begin to imagine. We are more than our weight, ability, or any diagnoses. And yet, these become the barometer of our health. If we decide to go along with that expectation, what other parts of our sense of wellness will slip through the cracks as we begin to obsess over solely our physical selves?

Regardless of our weight, ability, or diagnoses, it is likely that many of us have seen our society's emphasis on the physical. As a result, we've focused all of our mental and emotional energy toward the physical components of health and left our other forms of health and wellness in the dark. If you're anything like me, these experiences have led to profoundly complicated relationships with our own bodies. We've been conditioned to think of the thing that allows us to physically exist in the world as an enemy to be conquered or a defect to be corrected.

Your body is a magical thing, and it is beautiful. We've been told a false ideal and our minds and self-image have paid the price. A supposedly perfectly healthy body does not a healthy person make if it cost all the love they had for themself. But what does a cupcake cookbook know anyway? Let's ask my friend Maria, a nutritional scientist. Take it away, Maria!

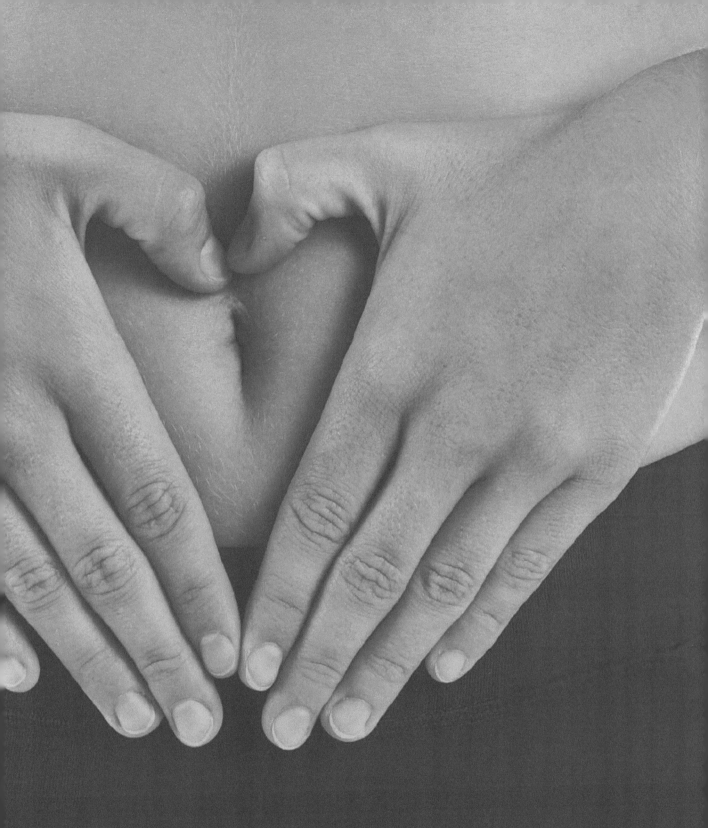

Contributed by

MARIA CAULEY, MS

Human Nutritional Scientist

Five Things More Important For You to Know Than Your Body Mass Index

#1 BMI IS TRASH.

If you aren't aware, Body Mass Index (BMI) is a method used to assess someone's weight in relation to their height. It's used in the medical world as a health risk indicator, AKA—the probability that you will develop chronic diseases in relation to this measurement. I'm embarrassed to admit that in my seven years of higher education, I was never taught the origin or history surrounding BMI. In my experience, I was taught which were healthy BMIs and which were not - and conditioned to think that any "unhealthy" BMI was bad, for both individuals who were underweight, and those who were overweight.

Well, buckle up for the mini history lesson that you never asked for. It turns out that the concept of BMI, then called "l'homme moyen" [average man] was created by a fellow named Adolphe Quetelet, about two centuries ago in Europe. Quetelet studied Astronomy, Mathematics, Sociology, and Statistics, and if he were alive today, he would probably wear fedoras and think "The Office" was the best show on TV.

"L'homme moyen" was created to determine the typical size for a man. It was created for statistical purposes because he studied statistics, not nutrition. To make this measurement even more exclusive, the participants used for his studies consisted solely of men of Western European descent (which is neither the first nor last time white men decided they were the example with which all others should follow).

So what does this all mean?! First of all, I feel it's problematic that we are using a 200 year measurement as a determinant of health and one that wasn't intended to evaluate health in the first place. Additionally, if we do continue to use BMI, it is neither an inclusive measurement nor representation of bodies. Being based on Western European males, various populations are excluded, including women, people of color, transgender and gender nonconforming individuals, and those with disabilities.

So, should you base your health status solely on your BMI? I say no. Like many things, the BMI scale has a sexist and racist history that I encourage you to think critically about. Health and wellness are more than your weight and height. Health includes mental, emotional, and spiritual health as well, alongside an individual's ability to self-regulate, seek out social support when needed, and have the ability to make rational and informed decisions as they navigate the world with minimal interference.

Moral of the story: I hope you stop associating your worth with your weight or your BMI. I am more concerned with how you handle failure and loss, your ability to communicate your needs and desires in a healthy manner, how you cope with stress, and if you have a stable support system of family and friends to help you through your one, glorious life.

"Don't wait on your weight to live the life you want." -CeCe Olisa

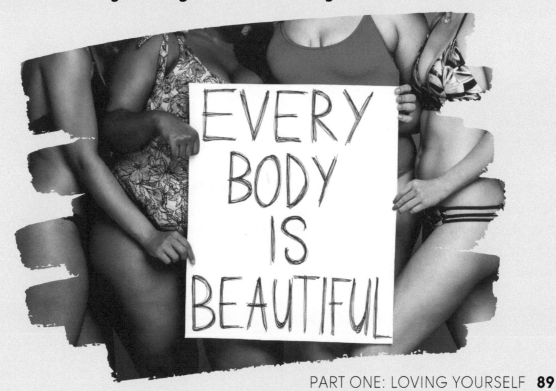

#2 YOUR BODY WAS MADE TO CHANGE.

Your body is going to change, regardless of what you want it to do (I know, that rebel.) Infancy, childhood, adolescence, and pregnancy are all examples of this. Even with this knowledge, I must admit to being a 25 year old who asks myself ~wHy mY clOtHeS fRom HigH SChoOL doN't FiT aNymORe~ Because Maria, you were a 14-year-old fetus who was still growing at that time.

Body changes are more than just weight loss or gain. As you age, your nutrient needs, metabolic rate, and hormone production alter. Additionally, life experiences, trauma, mental health status, and chronic illness can influence your daily habits and practices, which may manifest as physical changes in your body. All of the reasons above are valid and do not make your body inherently "good" or "bad"—just HUMAN. Next time you notice your body changing, just whisper "I see you lil' mama, way to go" and continue on with your day.

"Remember that our bodies are always changing, and that's okay. What's really unhealthy is trying to fit into an unrealistic norm of what is seen as perfect." -Olakemi

#3 SELF-LOVE & ACCEPTANCE ARE RADICAL.

A quick Google search revealed that the beauty and diet industry make $49 billion and $71 billion annually. This is impressive at an economic standpoint, but let's put on our critical thinking hats, okay? Collectively, these industries are profiting over $120 billion off of us hating ourselves—

which makes loving yourself, as you are, RADICAL AS HELL. 💯

Although I see these beauty standards as bogus, I still fall victim to them in the items I purchase and use: whitening toothpaste, vitamins, anti aging creams, Snapchat and Instagram filters, and expensive makeup that will make me look like a 2001 Bratz™ doll. Although I do desire to look like Yasmin, the philosophy behind these items is troublesome, as it adds to the myriad ways that we can hide from our authentic selves.

Did that last sentence sting a little, because it did for me. When was the last time you posted a selfie without a filter? Went to work without makeup? Put your money towards a company that uplifts you, rather than one that relies on you disapproving of your true self? Ah. now you understand how radical it is to love and accept yourself as you are.

"Thank U, Next" -Ariana Grande

#4 COMPARISON: THE TOXIC TRAIT YOU DIDN'T KNOW YOU HAD.

Sis, do you know how to log off of social media? I say this not to shame you, but to be transparent about my relationship with "staying connected". I noticed recently that I signed off so infrequently that I didn't know where the logout button on the app was, or what my password was to log back in. During this time, I found myself more isolated and self-critical than ever. Scrolling through engagement photoshoots, before-and-after weight loss posts, pregnancy announcements, and new homeowners next to their "SOLD" sign made me feel inadequate, to say the least.

People on social media put their best foot forward (myself included—accountability moment), which makes you feel like you're the only one with a mediocre credit score, stretch marks, an ingrown toenail, and $8 in savings (yes, that's me). None of the following are wrong, or something to feel shame about, but the social media narrative many of us have created in our minds beg to differ.

I encourage you to set some social media boundaries for yourself. This could include turning off notifications, unfollowing people who make you feel inadequate, or promising to post and share content that reflect you, authentically. When social media is used to compare, rather than connect, it can become toxic very quickly.

"Comparison is an act of violence against the self." -Iyanla Vanzant.

#5 DIETS EXPECT YOU TO FAIL.

Ouch, this one might sting a little, and that's okay.

There are hundreds of different diet programs out there, and they all seem promising and worth your money. (Side note: the diet industry is a business at the end of the day. They care about profit—not you having a healthy relationship with food and exercise). People fail at diets because they are not sustainable. Obsessing over macronutrients, counting calories in 7 sticks of carrots, and depriving yourself for the sake of being smaller are not realistic long-term changes. Additionally, many diet programs are owned and operated by doctors and business professionals, who have very little formal education on nutrition and human metabolism.

"You have been criticizing yourself for years and it hasn't worked. Try approving of yourself and see what happens." -Louise Hay

Lemon Lavender

SOUR & FLOWER, A TOTAL WOW-ER

Lemon and lavender is possibly one of my favorite flavor combos ever. The way that the floral lavender taste serves as a stunning crescendo to the tart lemon is a thing to behold. Plus, the calming properties of lavender can't be stated enough. These are both refreshing and relaxing, and you deserve a break.

Ingredients

CAKE

- 1 1/2 cups all-purpose flour
- 2 tsp. baking powder
- 1/2 tsp. salt
- 1/2 cup butter, softened
- 1 cup granulated sugar
- 2 large eggs, room temperature
- 1 tsp. vanilla extract
- 1 cup whole milk
- 2 tbsp. lemon zest
- 1/2 cup lemon juice
- A few drops of yellow food coloring for vibrancy (optional)

FROSTING

- 1 cup butter, softened
- 4-5 cups confectioner's sugar
- 2 tsp. finely chopped culinary lavender flowers
- 1 tsp. pure vanilla extract
- 1 tbsp. heavy cream
- A few drops lavender extract, to amplify flavor (optional)
- A few drops of food coloring, purple or mixing red and blue together) for a subtle lavender shade (optional)
- Lemon curd (optional)

Relaxation is good for you...

You deserve to rest without guilt or shame that your time was not spent "productively." Taking the time for yourself is not selfish, it's basic survival! If you don't let yourself recharge, you won't be fully present for the moments that matter anyway.

Instructions

- Preheat oven to 350°F and fill your cupcake tin with desired cupcake papers or liners.
- For the cake, sift and mix flour, baking powder, and salt. In another bowl, cream together the butter and sugar, mixing well before adding eggs and vanilla and mixing again until well combined.
- Slowly incorporate the dry mixture to the wet mixture in portions, mixing each time. When all of the dry mixture is incorporated, add milk, lemon zest, and lemon juice. If being used, add coloring as well. Mix until just combined.
- Pour batter into baking cups until each is about 3/4 full. Bake for approximately 20-22 minutes or until an inserted toothpick comes out clean. Cool before frosting.
- To make frosting, cream butter until smooth before gradually adding confectioner's sugar until the desired consistency is achieved. When close to the desired consistency, add heavy cream, flowers and vanilla, as well as optional coloring and lavender extract if you are using them. Add coloring in very small increments, especially if a subtle and soft shade of lavender is desired. Add additional heavy cream or milk to thin as needed for consistency.
- When cupcakes have cooled, pipe lavender buttercream on your cupcakes. If a stronger lemon flavor is desired, fill cupcakes or brush the top with optional lemon curd before piping your buttercream. Garnish with a sprinkling of additional chopped lavender flowers or other garnishes you may want, such as whole edible flowers for a powerful floral decoration.

Makes approximately one dozen cupcakes.

Recipe adapted from Bake du Jour | www.bakedujour.com

There's only one you on this planet.

With billions of people in this world and more every day, you are infinitely precious.

You are a rare treasure worth protecting.

96

Shoot, I'm Out of Sugar.

How are we supposed to make the world a sweeter place if our jar of sugar is empty?

To be human is to be fallible. One of our many imperfections is that we find ourselves having finite amounts of physical, mental, and emotional energy. With having such an important resource be limited like that, it's imperative that we go about our lives in ways that are intentional about how we distribute and budget that energy how we want.

As I've mentioned earlier, you can't pour from an empty cup. If we want to be able to emit positivity and love into the world, we have to make sure that we have the energy to do it.

Your cup is precious. Think about this theoretical cup that contains your emotional and mental energies with which you sip love from and offer to others. Tell me about it. Is it a mug? A glass? A mason jar? Is it decorated with anything, like maybe a funny or affirming quote to help you make it through the day? For me, I modeled my own after a cup given to me by my neighbor that says "Enjoy Life, Eat Cake." Keep thinking about that cup and just give it a warm and loving smile as you acknowledge it. That cup protects a very important resource for you, and we appreciate that cup so much for doing so. In addition, we can be intentional about our methods and the way we go about our days to show our cups that the appreciation goes beyond words and into concrete action.

A common buzz-word that many of us see from time to time is "self-care." As the name explicitly suggests, these are the techniques or strategies with which we take care of ourselves. With the recent popularity of this concept of self-care, I think it's important to note that many of the discussions of what self-care is and looks like have been heavily skewed by that very popularity that sparked the initial conversation.

Earlier, it was mentioned about how things like social media are always a "best foot forward" and act as a highlight reel. Similarly with self-care, many of the ways we talk about and see self-care have been focused toward only the side of the conversation that looks good on Instagram.

Now don't get me wrong, I would be lying if I said I wasn't also incredibly enthusiastic about the candlelit bubble baths and binge marathons of my favorite shows. I would also be lying if I said that those things weren't important. They are, but there's more to it.

There's more than one way to take care of ourselves and balance is vital. Self-care absolutely can be those special treats for yourself after a long day. However, self-care isn't always as glamorous. Sometimes self-care is literally rolling out of your bed to take a shower or eat something because it's 5pm and you haven't left your bed yet. Sometimes it's doing a week of dishes you've been putting off because you've run out of clean dishes to use. Sometimes self-care is joyful, but sometimes it's downright miserable. The twist is that both are equally important.

The way I help myself distinguish the two concepts is self-care versus soul-care. Self-care for me is those very basic things I can accomplish that meet my basic needs and allow me to continue functioning as a person. They may not be very fun, but they also keep me alive and that's important. On the flip side, soul-care becomes those tasks that fulfill you and restore you in a more emotional or mental way, rather than physical. You may also find some things fulfill both your self-care and your soul-care, and that's absolutely fabulous!

Just like when we talked about health, this is all about balance. We can't focus on our physical health at the expense of our mental or emotional wellbeing and vice versa. Similarly, we can't pit our self-care and soul-care against each other with a winner-takes-all mentality and only cater to one.

Sometimes, you'll find that self-care takes priority over soul-care, and vice versa. That's how it goes sometimes. But having a solid balance of both is an efficient way to restore our energies and maintain any current reserves.

Another way to look at our physical, mental, and emotional needs is an acronym that I was introduced to during my therapist training. Originally H.A.L.T. and introduced to me as H.A.L.T.O., this acronym breaks down the basic needs most humans have so that you're able to check in with yourself. H.A.L.T. was originated in Alcoholics Anonymous (A.A.) groups, and the first documented record of it was in a publication by Barry Leach in 1975. Here's what the letters mean:

H - Hungry: Have you eaten recently? Making sure that we have food in our bodies and that we're nourished can be important for our ability to function. If your "H" is present, maybe it's time to take a break and find yourself some food.

A - Angry: Are you finding yourself angry, upset, or feeling activated about something? Especially in an emotional or mental sense, feelings of anger can cloud our judgment and ability to think clearly. If you find yourself with an "A," take a second to cool down and let your emotions out in an appropriate way.

L - Lonely: We're social creatures! If we're feeling lonely, that can profoundly affect our emotional and mental stability. If your "L" is showing up, reach out to a friend or loved one or find another way to address your feelings of loneliness.

T - Tired: Have you been sleeping enough? If you're not rested, this once again will compromise your wellbeing. Take a nap or get some rest if your "T" is making itself known.

O - Orgasm: This is a newer addition to the acronym that I first heard from professor Dr. Markie Twist when I was in one of their courses learning to be a sex therapist. For many people, their needs for physical intimacy or sexual release can have just as much of an impact on their present state as any of the other components. If your "O" is getting your attention, do what you gotta do. There's no shame in getting your needs taken care of. Especially when you're in a context where you can get those needs met in a way that's appropriate for the situation and consensual for all involved, why deny yourself the fulfillment?

When it comes to H.A.L.T.O. and your needs, try not to panic and get overwhelmed. It's not some game of whack-a-mole where you need to address every single little thing that ever comes up. In fact, most people can usually function fine if one is needing to be addressed. Two, on the other hand, starts to become more concerning. Three or more should really be taken care of if you have the chance to address it.

Sources: Leach, B. (1975). Living sober. Alcoholics Anonymous World Services.
Twist, M.L.C. (n.d.). "H.A.L.T.O. checklist." University of Wisconsin-Stout, Fall 2018. Class handout.

Part Two

LOVING
OTHERS

First and foremost, I feel the deep need to tell you something. I'm so immensely proud of you. Even if we've never met and I have no idea you're reading this book, my heart is glowing for you. You made it through the first part of this book and, in many ways, one of the hardest. You've done the work and you should be proud of yourself just as much as I am.

Think of that first part as a springboard as it launches us into this next bit of work. Many of the very same concepts of self-kindness can be applicable to our relationships with others. In addition to those concepts, this part of the book will add in the other considerations that would be needed to navigate our relationships with other people. With each person, they bring their own sets of contexts, backgrounds, beliefs, and perspectives that need to be considered. Along with adding new ideas about ways to be loving and kind, we'll add some more recipes along the way that are a little more complicated but also add significant "wow" factor.

One final note before we get started: I'll be talking at length about "relationships" and I want to make an important distinction. Humans are relational, social creatures. While our romantic relationships with our intimate partners or spouses are definitely important relationships to consider when doing this work, we have so many relationships in our lives. We have relationships with friends, family, colleagues, coworkers, roommates, community members, and so many more. So, think of them too when you work toward sweeter, kinder, and more loving relationships.

Love is a limitless resource, let's sprinkle it everywhere.

Living is more than just breathing.

Trees take in carbon dioxide and fill the world with air, supporting life on the planet.

We hold the power to receive love and give it in return, a cycle as deep and magnificent as the roots of the tallest and oldest trees.

The trees may support life with their air, but our ability to give and receive love is an infinite rotation only bested by the stars... and it's what makes life worth living.

Your existence is a breath of fresh air.

Love is a Two-Way Sweet

Expressing love with a cupcake is great, but it's sweeter when you know it's their favorite flavor.

You know the sayings: it takes two to tango, it takes two to make a thing go right, and the list goes on. What it's trying to get at here is that in relationships where people are interacting with each other, we're juggling twice as many balls in the air when we reflect on how we communicate.

When we're reflecting on our own thoughts, we've got the whole recipe in front of us. We can take into consideration our mood, our thought patterns, our upbringing, and a million other things as to what got us having those thoughts.

When we bring another person into the equation, it's like the recipe is cut in half and you have the ingredients and they have the instructions. We know exactly how much of what goes into the recipe, but we don't know how we use the ingredients or in what order. The other person will have the same problem seeing exactly how to make what the recipe is for but have absolutely no idea how much of anything goes into it. In our conversations and relationships, the ingredients and instructions get replaced with our own individual thoughts, contexts, experiences, perspectives, and intentions.

We own our unique perspectives and contexts which is what allows us to bring them to the table in our relationships with others. For good reason, we don't own other people's perspectives and contexts when we interact, which is why they are the only person who can bring them to the table. Moral of the story, we can only own the things we bring to the table ourselves, and everyone else brings their own stuff. We only get the full picture when we each bring ourselves to the table and share what we bring with others, like some amazing and intimate emotional potluck where we all come together.

Think of a potluck you've been to. There are those dishes someone brings and they're absolutely LEGENDARY. For me, it was my godfather's lemon cheesecake at family get-togethers growing up (which definitely inspired one of my best cupcake recipes which you'll get to in a few pages). What's yours? Maybe someone brings mac 'n' cheese you'd swear was liquid gold. Maybe a it's a casserole that causes you to weep tears of joy just by smelling it. Maybe it's a potato salad that tastes like god herself made it, or maybe it's a pie so good that you'd make Nicolas Cage stealing the Declaration of Independence look like an amateur as you try to get your hands on the recipe.

We all have that legendary potluck contribution that we can think of. And we are all-too-familiar with the eventual realization that nothing we do will ever recreate it. There's something special the originator puts into it that we'll never be able to duplicate. Similarly, the perspectives we bring into our relationships will always be our own, and theirs will always be theirs. And no matter how hard we try, we can't recreate each other's recipes for ourselves.

As with any good potluck or similar event (I personally love me a good brunch), proper planning and communication is essential to make sure everyone is fully able to enjoy the experience of sharing food and friendship together. For example, checking ahead for things like allergy or diet considerations is vital to make sure that everyone is safe and will be able to eat. If I'm having a bunch of my vegan and gluten-free friends over for brunch (a distant fantasy as I write this book in ye-olde-times-of-COVID), I wouldn't try to serve them all huge stacks of pancakes, a golden platter of cream cheese pastries, and literal pounds of bacon. Personally, I think such a brunch sounds absolutely divine. That's my perspective, not theirs.

Communication like this is important because it helps us establish a culture of mutual respect and consideration within our relationships. Regardless of how it comes up, these communications need to happen. In this brunch example, maybe those friends will tell me in advance that they're vegan and gluten-free so that I make sure everything is good to go come brunch day. If they don't, then I have the obligation as the brunch planner to make sure that I've checked with everyone and know what everyone needs. Especially if I reach out and communicate, it shows to them that I care, and that I value our relationship enough to make sure that I'm being conscious and considerate of what they're needing and not imposing what I would think the answer might be for them.

My mom always told me "You know what assuming does." I'm not going to spell it out for you but it's not good. So let's not do that in our relationships and assume that we get right away what something means. Don't take "I want brunch" and assume it means bacon. When your loved ones bring something to the table, don't assume further details of what that means for them. Besides, asking is a great way to build intimacy.

If you take anything away from this potluck/brunch, besides leftovers, just remember that we are complex creatures with various contexts, perspectives, intentions, and needs. These things are also constantly changing for all of us, as well as for those we find ourselves having relationships with. Just as it's vital that we consistently check in with ourselves, we should be checking in with our friends and family too. They grow and change just as we do and that's profoundly amazing.

Sometimes people will bring the tried-and-true recipes they know work, but sometimes people will find a new recipe that they want to try out and bring that instead. Also, who was able to make it this time might not be all the same people who are able to make it next time. No single potluck will ever look exactly the same, and neither will our conversations or interactions with those in our lives. If we don't make sure to keep checking in and communicating, we might bring something someone is allergic to and cause unintended harm for someone we care about.

Sometimes keeping track of who's allergic to what or what people like and don't like can be a lot to keep track of, just like what our various loved ones bring to the table from their own perspectives and contexts. It's hard work, but it's so important.

Lemon Cheesecake

HAPPINESS IN A CUPCAKE

This cupcake reminds me about keeping your loved ones close. I based this recipe off the treat my godfather is known for bringing to family get-togethers. I also think of one of my best friends, Emily, who was in my cohort for my therapy degree in grad school. This cupcake is her favorite.

Ingredients

CAKE

- 2 cups all-purpose flour
- 1 1/2 tsp. baking powder
- 1/2 tsp. baking soda
- 1 tsp. salt
- 10 tbsp. butter, room temp
- 1 1/4 cups granulated sugar
- 3 large eggs
- 1 tsp. vanilla extract
- 2/3 cup milk
- 3 tbsp. grated lemon zest
- 1/3 cup fresh lemon juice
- Yellow gel coloring, for vibrancy (optional)

When life gives you lemons...

You're here, which means you've made it through everything you've faced until now. All of your life is story after story of you surviving each twist. Whatever comes next, you're more capable to face it than you've ever realized before.

FROSTING

- 8 tbsp. butter, room temp
- 8 oz. cream cheese, room temp
- 2-4 cups confectioner's sugar, more or less to taste and for consistency
- Heavy cream or milk as needed to thin
- 1 tbsp. vanilla extract, more or less to taste
- Sprinkle of salt to taste

FILLING & TOPPING

- Small jar lemon curd (or homemade if preferred)
- 8 oz. cream cheese, softened
- 1/2 cup heavy whipping cream
- 1/4 cup granulated sugar
- 2 tsp. confectioner's sugar
- 1 1/2 tbsp. sour cream
- 1 tsp. lemon juice
- 1/2 tsp. vanilla extract

- If making your own lemon curd, make in advance.
- Preheat oven to 350°F and fill your cupcake tin with desired cupcake papers or liners.
- To get started on the cake, combine sugar and lemon zest so the zest is coated with sugar, by hand or in a food processor.
- Combine milk and lemon juice in a separate bowl and let sit while working on other ingredients.
- Sift your dry ingredients: flour, baking powder, baking soda, and salt, and whisk together until well combined.
- Cream butter before adding the lemon sugar mixture with a hand or stand mixer. When combined, add one egg and mix again, continuing with the remaining eggs one at a time. Add vanilla.
- Add 1/3 of the dry ingredients to the mixer and combine. Then follow with half of the milk mixture and combine. Repeat so the order of adding to the mix is dry, milk, dry, milk, dry. When finally combined, add coloring if you want a rich yellow shade.
- Pour batter into baking cups until approximately 3/4 full and then bake approximately 35 minutes or until an inserted toothpick comes out clean.
- While cupcakes are baking, begin making filling by whipping cream until stiff peaks form.
- In another bowl, combine cream cheese, both sugars, sour cream, lemon juice, and vanilla until well combined. Fold in whipped cream and transfer to a piping bag. Chill in the refrigerator until ready to use.
- Make frosting by creaming butter and cream cheese together before gradually adding confectioner's sugar until the desired consistency is reached. Add vanilla and salt for flavor. Thin with milk or cream as needed. Transfer to piping bag with desired tip.
- Assemble by removing the center of a cooled cupcake with a small knife or apple corer. Fill with filling. Brush top with curd before piping frosting. Garnish with graham cracker crumbs or lemon zest/slices as desired.

Makes approximately one dozen cupcakes.

Cake recipe adapted from John Kanell of Preppy Kitchen | www.preppykitchen.com
Filling recipe adapted from Sally's Baking Addiction | www.sallysbakingaddiction.com

Root Beer Float

CARBONATED CONFECTION

I loved root beer floats as a kid. So simple, but so tasty. What else do you need to justify these cupcakes? For me, the sentimental value to these cupcakes doesn't stop at the favored childhood treat. Much of my desire to bake with fun and creative flavors in mind came from when I would be in the kitchen with my mom. My first introduction to the root beer float cupcake was when my mom and I brainstormed the idea and made them together. This recipe is exactly how we would make them, and it only made sense to keep that going as an adult. These ones are for you, mom.

Ingredients

CAKE

- 2 1/2 cups all-purpose flour
- 2 1/2 tsp. baking powder
- 1/2 tsp. salt
- 3/4 cup butter, softened
- 1 1/2 cup granulated sugar
- 3 large eggs, room temperature
- 1 tbsp. root beer extract
- 1/2 tsp. pure vanilla extract
- 1 cup root beer

GARNISH

- 1/2 cup root beer barrel candies, crushed

FROSTING

- 1 batch vanilla buttercream, set aside (see pages 72 & 73)
- 1 cup butter, softened
- 3 cups confectioner's sugar
- 3 tbsp. root beer
- 1 tsp. root beer extract
- 1 tsp. pure vanilla extract
- A few drops of brown and/or orange gel food coloring

Root-tine Reminders...

The wonderful thing about telling people that you love them is that it appears to be a renewable resource and it takes so little to do it. Since this recipe was for my mom and she's someone I could always say I love more, I'll go first: Hey mom, if you're reading this, I love you!

- Preheat oven to 350°F and fill your cupcake tin with desired cupcake papers or liners.
- For the cake, begin by sifting flour, salt, and baking powder into a medium bowl before whisking together. In another bowl, or your mixer, cream together butter and sugar.
- Once butter and sugar are well combined and fluffy, add eggs, root beer, and pure vanilla extract mix until combined.
- Gradually add flour mixture and root beer to batter, alternating between the two in manageable increments.
- Pour batter into baking cups until approximately 3/4 full and then bake approximately 20 minutes or until an inserted toothpick comes out clean. Allow to fully cool.
- While cupcakes are baking, make vanilla buttercream according to recipe on pages 72 and 73 before beginning to make root beer frosting.
- Make root beer frosting by creaming butter, root beer extract, and vanilla before gradually adding confectioner's sugar until the desired consistency is reached. Add root beer. If frosting thins too much, add more confectioner's sugar. Add gel food coloring until frosting is a light shade that is reminiscent of root beer and just dark enough to contrast with the vanilla buttercream but isn't too saturated.
- Assemble your piping bag and fill one side of bag with one frosting and the opposite side with the other frosting. Pipe a small amount of frosting out of your bag onto a plate or napkin to get both colors flowing. This will create a striping effect when frosting your cupcakes.
- Finish your cooled cupcakes by piping the vanilla/root beer frostings on top and garnish with crushed root beer barrels.

Makes approximately one dozen cupcakes.

Recipe adapted from Cincy Shopper | www.cincyshopper.com

We are containers with which we can fill love and kindness.

Just as we are beautifully diverse in so many ways, it is natural that our containers can be different shapes and sizes.

Needing more love to feel full doesn't make you a container that is broken or leaking— just one that is different.

That's okay.

Wait, I Thought it was in Metric?

Listing your ingredients without amounts or measurements is a recipe for disaster.

Remember that analogy we talked about earlier where someone has the ingredients of a recipe and the other person has the instructions? It's time to break that down a bit more and talk about how we can make sure that we all have what we need to whip up some love and kindness together.

Think about if you're baking with someone this way and you're not allowed to tell each other what's on your half of the recipe or help each other. Think of all the different possibilities of how it could go horribly wrong. What was the worst part of this mayhem? I'm guessing it wasn't necessarily that the recipe was split in half, but it was that you weren't able to work together with the respective halves and fill in the gaps for each other. When we're navigating our relationships, we aren't able to know what's on the other person's recipe unless we communicate.

One of the most common ways that this issue of not having each other's recipes comes up is the ways in which we express love and appreciation. We as humans have various different ways to express love and appreciation and—naturally—we all have differing opinions about which ones we like best. Not only that, but it gets even more complicated when we talk about preferences for giving versus receiving love.

One of the best ways that this concept has been broken down is with the five love languages, which was first introduced in the 1990s by Dr. Gary Chapman when he first wrote his best-selling book that laid them all out.

The five love languages are as follows: Words of Affirmation, Acts of Service, Giving/Receiving Gifts, Quality Time, and Physical Touch. I'm no Dr. Chapman, but I'll lay them out for you with what I know best—baking cupcakes.

Source: Chapman, G. D. (1995). *The five love languages: How to express heartfelt commitment to your mate.* Chicago: Northfield Pub.

Words of Affirmation:

"You're so good at baking cupcakes. I think this is your best flavor yet!"

Acts of Service:

"You've been baking all day and you're probably really tired. Let me take care of the dishes for you."

Giving/Receiving Gifts:

"Hey, I know you've been baking more often so I got you a new stand mixer because I thought it might help you out!"

Quality Time:

"How about we share some cupcakes and snuggle on the couch while we catch up on that show we've been watching?"

Physical Touch:

"Wanna cuddle and I'll rub your back while you wait for those cupcakes to cool?"

The introduction of these love languages has been absolutely revolutionary in helping us better understand ways to express our wants and needs. For each of those love languages, we all have our individual preferences for which ones we like the most and least when it comes to expressing love. It's also important to note that we may have similar or different preferences when we make the distinction of how we like to express love and how we want to receive it in return. One that I see commonly, which may be a Midwest humility thing, is that many of us like to give gifts to others but feel uncomfortable or unsure of what to say when we ourselves are the ones to receive a gift.

Looking at the list of love languages, you can probably get a good idea already of what ones you probably gravitate more and less toward. There's also a wide variety of online quizzes that you can take to figure out a more exact breakdown of your favorite to least favorite ways to give and receive love.

When we're engaging with people in our lives, it's important that we're being considerate of how they want our love for them to be expressed. As we've discussed throughout our reflections on our relationships, imposing our own ideas or perspectives on each other can lead to relationship strain that easily could have been avoided if we had just communicated.

For many of us, if there's a love language we don't gravitate toward as much, we may not even notice in the moment that it is intended as an expression of love, which could leave the sender feeling burned and hurt.

If we have a recipe that uses measurements we don't have the tools for, we need to spend the deliberate and intentional time converting those measurements. Some of them may be easy, like if your tablespoon broke but you know that one tablespoon is three teaspoons so you're fine. But maybe you have some more difficult conversions, like having to find out that one cup is about 236.59 mL in metric (and YES, I did have to look that up on the internet because I'm HUMAN and the U.S. education system has failed us all by not getting us all to just switch to metric in the first place).

The point here is that—as with many things in our relationships—these extra steps and communication take time and effort on all sides. However, I cannot begin to describe the degree of how priceless and profoundly important those extra little things are to our ability to foster stronger and more loving relationships.

Chocolate Chip

IT'LL "DOUGH" YOUR MIND

This cupcake is a game changer and I also based them off of my fiancé's favorite treat, chocolate chip cookies. When I began stocking up my metaphorical rolodex of flavors, I knew chocolate chip would be one, especially after my friend Meghan introduced me to her cookie dough frosting recipe which was a total game changer. If you were told not to lick the spoon as a kid because of the raw eggs, this cupcake is a guaranteed way to make up for lost time and get that cookie dough fix risk-free.

Ingredients

CAKE

- 2 3/4 cups all-purpose flour
- 1 1/2 cups light brown sugar, packed tightly
- 1 1/2 tsp. baking powder
- 1/2 tsp. baking soda
- 1/2 tsp. salt
- 10 tbsp. softened unsalted butter, cut into small cubes
- 3 large eggs
- 1 1/3 cup buttermilk
- 2 tsp. vanilla extract
- 1 cup mini chocolate chips

FILLING

- 1/2 cup baking chocolate
- 1/2 cup heavy cream or milk

FROSTING

- 1 cup butter, softened
- 3/4 cup brown sugar
- 1 cup confectioner's sugar
- 1 cup flour
- 2 tsp. vanilla
- 1/2 tsp. salt
- 1/8 - 1/4 cup milk depending on desired consistency
- 1 cup mini chocolate chips

Never enough spoons to lick...

A common metaphor in disability and mental health circles is having a finite amount of "spoons" to spend throughout the day, meaning a limited amount of emotional energy you can expend on daily tasks or interactions. Give yourself permission to say, "Hey, I just simply don't have the capacity to do this right now."

Instructions

- Ahead of your baking, make chocolate ganache filling by putting your baking chocolate and heavy cream/milk in a saucepan on low to medium heat. Stir occasionally until chocolate is melted and the mixture is well combined. Cool ganache and let set in the fridge.
- To make the cupcakes, preheat oven to 350°F and fill your cupcake tin with desired cupcake papers or liners.
- For the cake, sift flour, sugar, baking powder, baking soda, and salt into your mixing bowl. Whisk dry ingredients until well combined.
- In a separate bowl, combine eggs, buttermilk, and vanilla.
- Incorporate butter into your dry ingredients. Use a slow speed and add butter in increments. The final result should look crumbly. Scrape the sides of your bowl to make sure you get everything mixed.
- Add your egg mixture in halves, beating until you have a thick batter.
- Fold in the chocolate chips and then add batter to baking cups until cups are 3/4 full before baking for 30-35 minutes or until an inserted toothpick comes out clean or with minimal crumbs attached. Look closely as melted chocolate may also resemble uncooked batter.
- While cupcakes are baking, begin the frosting by creaming together the brown sugar, confectioner's sugar, and softened butter at a low speed.
- Add flour, salt and vanilla then mix on medium speed until the frosting is creamy and flour is well incorporated, using milk as necessary.
- Fold chocolate chips into frosting mixture. If you are piping your frosting rather than spreading it, skip this step to avoid clogging your piping tip with chocolate chips.
- When cupcakes are cooled, cut out middles with a small knife or apple corer and fill with chocolate ganache. Spread frosting and chocolate chip mixture on your filled cupcakes or pipe frosting on your filled cupcakes followed by generously sprinkling with mini chocolate chips.

Makes approximately one dozen cupcakes.

Cake recipe adapted from My Cake School | www.mycakeschool.com
Frosting recipe courtesy of Meghan Lueck, adapted from twosisterscrafting.com

New York Cheesecake

YOU CAN CAKE IT ANYWHERE

This cupcake idea was born out of a specific request. When I was bringing cupcakes to an bonfire, they said a favorite dessert was New York Style cheesecake. The rest is history. Bada bing, bada boom.

Ingredients

CAKE

- 2 large eggs, separated
- 2 1/4 cups all-purpose flour
- 2 1/2 tsp. baking powder
- 1/2 tsp. salt
- 3/4 cup butter, softened
- 1 3/4 cups granulated sugar
- 3 tsp. pure vanilla extract
- 1 cup whole milk

The best cheesecake jiggles...

If you find some excess energy in your body from being upset or angry or hurt, shake it out. Many animals will shake off excess energy when they've recently escaped becoming a meal. This gets that excess energy from fight or flight mode out of their body. We can do the same.

FROSTING

- 8 tbsp. butter, room temperature
- 8 oz. cream cheese, room temperature
- 2-4 cups confectioner's sugar, more or less to taste and for consistency
- Heavy cream or milk as needed to thin
- 1 tbsp. vanilla extract, more or less to taste
- Sprinkle of salt to taste

FILLING & TOPPING

- Fruit topping of choice (strawberries, blueberries, cherries, combination, etc.)
- 8 oz. cream cheese, softened
- 1/2 cup heavy whipping cream
- 1/4 cup granulated sugar
- 2 tsp. confectioner's sugar
- 1 1/2 tbsp. sour cream
- 1 tsp. lemon juice
- 1/2 tsp. vanilla extract
- 1 cup graham cracker crumbs

Instructions

- If making your own fruit topping, make in advance.
- Preheat oven to 350°F and fill your cupcake tin with desired cupcake papers or liners.
- To get started on the cake, beat egg whites until soft peaks form then set aside. Sift flour, baking powder, and salt in another bowl and whisk together until combined.
- Cream butter then add sugar, mixing until well combined. Add egg yolks and vanilla and mix again.
- Add dry ingredients and whole milk to your mixture in portions, alternating between them and both starting and ending with the dry ingredients. After dry ingredients and milk are fully incorporated, gently fold in the whipped egg whites.
- Pour batter into baking cups until approximately 3/4 full and then bake approximately 18-21 minutes or until a toothpick comes out clean. Allow to cool fully.
- While cupcakes are baking, begin making filling by whipping cream until stiff peaks form.
- In another bowl, combine cream cheese, both sugars, sour cream, lemon juice, and vanilla until well combined. Fold in whipped cream and transfer to a piping bag. Chill in the refrigerator until ready to use.
- Make frosting by creaming butter and cream cheese together before gradually adding confectioner's sugar until the desired consistency is reached. Add vanilla and salt for flavor. Thin with milk or cream as needed. Transfer to piping bag with desired tip.
- Assemble by removing the center of a cooled cupcake with a small knife or apple corer. Fill with filling. Spread a thin layer of frosting to seal in the filling. Then begin to pipe a swirl of frosting but instead create a slightly tall ring or well of frosting, rather than the normal peak-type shape of piped frosting. Fill the well with your fruit topping of choice then sprinkle the rim of the cupcake with graham cracker crumbs.

Makes approximately 12-16 cupcakes.

Cake & Filling recipes adapted from Sally's Baking Addiction | www.sallysbakingaddiction.com

Knowing that we are capable of harm to ourselves and others is reason for intentional consideration and deliberate responsibility.

Knowing that we are capable of fostering healing for ourselves and others is reason for great relief and wonderous passion.

We are profoundly capable of both harm and healing, and one cannot exist without the other.

We cannot heal pain without acknowledgement of the harm that was done, just as we cannot avoid further harm if we do not allow the healing process to begin.

Oh, You Had Called Dibs on That?

When the negotiations over the last cupcake have failed (someone already ate it) and we need diplomatic solutions to ease the tension.

We've all been there. We wanted the last cupcake, the last appetizer, the last fry in the bag, you get the picture. We say that we'll take it if no one wants it, but make sure to not seem too eager. Then, in a dramatic plot twist, some fool who didn't hear us goes in and snags it before we know what hit us. We start seeing red and we can hear dramatic alarm-esque music in the background of our minds.

Not only have we been in that position, but I'm sure that many of us also have been that fool who didn't even realize our hubris in clearing the platter before we suddenly become deer in headlights at the sound of "Hey, who took the last one?"

So how do we prevent these things from escalating and involved parties preparing for all-out war? Having likely been in both positions before, I'm sure we can have some deep and profound "bigger picture" perspective of the whole ordeal?

Did you answer, "They didn't hear them claim it and wouldn't have eaten it if they knew it was spoken for?" Congratulations! You've guessed correctly and I hope that wherever you are, you hear triumphant game show victory music and the stage rotates to highlight your fabulous prize. As the golden curtains open, confetti rains from the ceiling and a banner is revealed which reads "Congratulations, you have critical thinking skills." This isn't even sarcasm. As social media comment sections have shown me the past several years, critical thinking is a rare and underappreciated trait.

Seeing both sides of this situation from our outside perspective, we know that someone's claim was not honored and someone else caused harm without even realizing what they were doing. There was no malice whatsoever—just a simple misunderstanding that ended with accidental transgressions.

This, my friends, leads us to the discussion of intention versus impact, and how we can be mindful of both in our relationships.

Intent and impact are two sides of a coin in a situation, and looking at both can give us a sense of the bigger picture. Let's look back at that scenario from earlier with the last cupcake or appetizer. The impact, what happened, is that harm was caused and someone was upset when something they had claimed was taken. The intent, which is what we're wanting to happen (or a lack of considering what might happen) when going into a situation, was that the other person was completely unaware that someone else had claimed the last one.

Intent can make a big difference in a situation. Imagine how that scenario would look vastly different if the intent had been more deliberate. Maybe they had heard the other person claim it, but grabbed it to spite them because some undisclosed (but likely very juicy) drama between the two. Whatever the underlying reasons, a more deliberate and spiteful intention in clearing the platter would make this scenario an entirely different story. That's why intent is important to consider when we're navigating the complexities of healing when harm is done.

However, there's one caveat that's important to note. Intent has the ability to paint a whole different story, but it can't change the genre of the book. If harm is done, that's that. A toxic trait I've seen far too often is to assert that people should not claim harm when the intent was benign. If your truth is that something has harmed you, no one can take that truth away from you.

I am thankful to have seen many conversations in recent years that have discussed this issue of intent and impact and how the impact someone experiences is an immutable truth of their reality in that moment. Regardless of intention, we have to acknowledge the impact of our actions if we are to have relationships with others that foster love and healing.

It's also important to note in these recent conversations that the focus on impact is important for those affected to speak their truth. However, we also must be careful to not swing the pendulum all the way to the opposite direction. Opposite of the aforementioned assertions that impact can be ignored in cases of benign intent, there is also the possibility of similarly toxic patterns where we assert that a benign intent cannot be claimed when harmful impact occurs. The intent of someone's actions is just as much their truth as the impacts being the truth of those they've affected. Neither truth can cancel out the other.

Just as we can't say "I didn't hear you claim the last one and wouldn't have taken it if I did, so you shouldn't be upset," we also cannot say "you were spiteful and took the last one to upset me." This deliberate denial of someone's truth will only attempt to mend harm by compounding more harm on top of it.

This example of fighting over a last cupcake or appetizer may seem silly, but it gives us a chance to understand these dynamics and considerations for when they come up in something more serious and complicated in our lives and relationships.

If we are hoping to have loving connections with others that focus on healing, we must recognize intent and impact as two truths that simultaneously exist together. Granted, our own individual needs may dictate that one has more focus at any given time and that's okay. It's normal in the immediate aftermath of harm to acknowledge that we can only focus on our own feelings and the impact for the moment. When we're ready and more capable, we can definitely come back to the conversation and look at the bigger picture of intent and impact in a way the conversation and our relationship deserves. If we're the person with the benign intent that didn't mean for the harm that's happened, just make sure to respect the requested space of the impacted person as they take their needed time. What will be vital for all involved is to make sure their truths don't speak for the others. Don't assert that someone you've impacted is overreacting, and speak for what the intentions must be of those who've done you harm. Neither of those things will foster a healing environment.

I tend to say that impact is for accountability and intent is for forgiveness. We need to acknowledge the impact of our actions if we are to hold ourselves accountable. Knowing someone's intent will inform us of how to move forward. Unintentional harm met with targeted anger as if it were deliberate will only infect our wounds and prevent clean healing. As for those who deliberately harm us, it's up to you on what boundaries you need to prevent further harm from them, and the terms with which that door would ever open again.

Buttercream Flowers

TURN OKAY INTO BOUQUET

Okay before I say literally anything else, here is your ONE chance in this book for pictures of cupcakes that I actually made (and I'm forever grateful to Sian for these GORGEOUS shots). Given that this section is all about a decoration rather than a recipe for a cupcake, I felt it was only fair to have a visual example here. Besides, I couldn't not use these pictures.

Let's talk for a second about where my floral frosting fixation all started. There's this shop in my town that I've been absolutely obsessed with ever since they first opened. It's a sustainable floral and gifts shop (Right? We love it.) owned by a remarkable woman named Sarah. Whenever I've needed flowers, I've gotten them from her. As I have written this book, she put together the flowers I gave to my now-fiancé on our first date, crafted a stunning floral crown and boutonnière for the formal event where he met many of my friends for the first time, and supplied the rose petals that adorned the stone steps where Jacob and I proposed to each other. Sarah is also definitely doing the flowers for our wedding. If she doesn't know that already, she'll know when she reads this book.

When I was first getting more serious about my cupcake baking, Sarah had been on a brief hiatus with the shop closed and reopening soon. I knew in my heart that I wanted to surprise her on the first day being back open with a bunch of floral cupcakes that she could celebrate with. I studied everything I could and likely have accumulated hundreds of hours and thousands of video views by now as I've practiced this craft. In addition, I've figured out some of my own tips and tricks along the way.

Now, here's your chance to create some beautiful floral frosting creations of your own. I also want to dedicate this section to Sarah. In celebrating how much she makes my community a sweeter place, I urge all of you reading this to support the local businesses that make your communities sweeter.

Photo: Sian Elizabeth Siska, Sian Elizabeth Photography | www.sianelizabethphotos.com

For the late bloomers...

There's no one single way we are supposed to grow, progress, or heal in our lives. Sometimes you may find the process to be a bit slower, and that is not a condemnation of you when other people go faster. You may even find the occasional step back in your journey. That's okay. Life isn't a linear process.

Getting Started

Before laying down your first petal, you'll want to do some planning. It's tedious, but this will make your life so much easier.

- Draft up what you want to do for your flowers. This will help make sure you have the correct tips, dyes, and figure out how much frosting you will want to make. If you're planning to do multiple different floral designs for an organic and natural feel when they're all together (extra work but so stunning and totally worth it when they're done), take some time to do the math and figure out how many of each design you want to do for your total number of cupcakes and draw up what you want the different designs to look like. This will help you not forget down the road.

- You should plan to at least have two different colors of frosting at a minimum—the flowers and the leaves. You may need more if you're doing multiple colors or if some flowers use different colors in the design.

- At minimum, make a 1.5 batch of buttercream with a slightly stiffer consistency. You can add extra salt to cut some of the sweetness if needed. Do not use cream cheese frosting as it won't hold shape as well and chocolate buttercream will be quite difficult to color. The 1.5 batch is for a dozen floral cupcakes with leaf and flower color. Add another half batch for each additional flower color you'll need. If you're only needing a small amount of another color, such as yellow for some of the centers, don't account for that extra color. That final batch number can then be modified for quantities other than a dozen, such as doubled if making two dozen cupcakes. That's a lot of math and I'm so sorry, so there's also a table down below that might be helpful too. It's not an exact science. As you get to larger quantities, you may be able to safely get away with less frosting, but it's better safe than sorry. If you're making a large quantity, it might be helpful to do a batch or two at a time.

	12 count	24 count	36 count
1 flower color	1.5 batch	3 batches	4.5 batches
2 flower colors	2 batches	4 batches	6 batches
3 flower colors	2.5 batches	5 batches	7.5 batches

Coloring Frosting

- Once buttercream is made, portion appropriately based on your planned colors. I usually do about 40% of the buttercream being reserved for the green leaf color and the remaining 60% gets split among my flower colors whether its one or multiple. As needed, set aside smaller portions for colors that won't be used as much, such as yellow for flower centers.

- As you color each portion of buttercream, it is recommended to go slow as to not oversaturate. It's much easier to add more color than take away color that was added too hastily.

- If you're trying to achieve very specific shades, looking at a reference photo (or even the real flowers if you have them around) can be really helpful. Try to determine what colors may help achieve the shade you're looking for. For example, just green food coloring can make leaves look really artificial, so I tend to add some brown and even red to my buttercream. Using a little bit of the opposite color on the color wheel will dull or mute your color without altering the shade like adding black or white food coloring to the mix would. Using the color wheel can also be helpful when trying to create shades you don't have by using other colors in your collection. If it helps, there's a flower with petals in the color wheel below to help you master your flower color artistry.

- Above all, make sure to have fun and play as you're coming up with your various colors. You're not some scientist trying to perfect a chemical formula and save the world, you're a magical force creating beautiful flora in the world that you want to see. Let the creative energies flow without restraint.

Tips (and Tricks)

 STANDARD: Round, circular opening. Comes in various widths. Smaller tips are good for writing or fine details like baby's breath, the center of small flowers, or vines.

 OPEN STAR: Pointed edges create an opening in the shape of an open star. Variations in length and width of points as well as number of points can create different effects. Useful for standard decorative piping and laying down small flowers.

 CLOSED STAR: Similar to an open star, but has slits rather than points, which create finer ribbons of piping. Useful for small flowers or creating roses by piping backwards and allowing the overlapping ribbons to look like petals.

 PETAL: Comes in various sizes and variations, including curved petals. As the name suggests, most useful for creating petals on a variety of flowers. Aiming with the thinner edge upward creates petals with a solid base and soft, delicate edges.

 CURVED RIBBON: This creates a ribbon of piping that curves in a half circle. Useful for creating overlapping patterns of curved petals in flowers like dahlias.

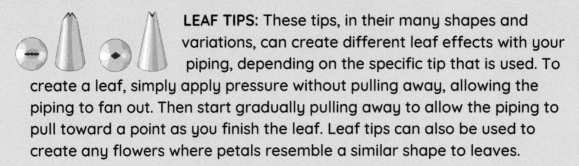 **LEAF TIPS:** These tips, in their many shapes and variations, can create different leaf effects with your piping, depending on the specific tip that is used. To create a leaf, simply apply pressure without pulling away, allowing the piping to fan out. Then start gradually pulling away to allow the piping to pull toward a point as you finish the leaf. Leaf tips can also be used to create any flowers where petals resemble a similar shape to leaves.

RUSSIAN PIPING TIPS: Last but not least is what we call "Russian Piping Tips," which are shown above. These differ from traditional piping tips as they are significantly larger and have a distinct flat top, where a pattern is cut out that can stamp a flower of piping. The pattern cut into the top will determine what type of flower or shape is created. These are fairly easy to use as you can simply apply some pressure to release some piping and then pull up and away ro release the flower that's now a part of your decorating!

Piping Flowers

Leaves

The first and most important piece of advice to offer is that, regardless of what flowers you're putting down, make sure to plan for some inclusion of leaves. Not only does adding leaves further enhance the natural and organic effect of your floral vision, but leaves also provide great filler for you where you can fill any gaps that wouldn't fit another flower as well as cover up any spots where you might have made a mistake or a flower didn't turn out like you wanted.

Simple Rose

Using a closed star tip, go in a reverse swirl motion that starts from the inside and moves outward. The thin ribbons will begin to overlap and resemble a rose. As you finish piping, aim your tip to tuck under the outermost edge of the rose for a cleaner edge. Cover seam with a leaf as needed.

Traditional Rose

For this flower, use of a flower nail and/or working on a separate work surface is helpful but not required. Using a petal tip with the wider edge at the bottom, create a small mound of piping to give your rose volume. Cover the top of the mound with a petal that wraps around it. Begin to form more petals around your preliminary petal with soft motions that curve gently upward and back down, like a small hill. Gradually increase the size of your petals as you expand outward, as well as start gradually moving lower to cover the bottoms of previous petals. In your last row or two of petals, make sure they have reached the bottom and are beginning to fan outward. If making this rose on a flower nail or separate work surface, remove from the nail gently and place on your cake or cupcake, or chill until needed. If you pipe directly on your dessert, ignore that step.

Rosebuds

Using a Russian piping tip with a rose petal cutout similar to the style shown on the left, apply pressure and lift up to stamp small rosebuds with your piping, repeating to lay a small cluster of small roses. Fill in gaps with leaves.

Small Flowers

Using an open or closed star tip, drop small flowers by simply stamping a small amount of piping in the desired location. Then use a small standard tip in a contrasting color to add centers to your small flowers with a simple dot of piping in the middle of the petals.

Large Flowers

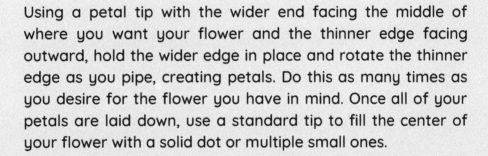

Using a petal tip with the wider end facing the middle of where you want your flower and the thinner edge facing outward, hold the wider edge in place and rotate the thinner edge as you pipe, creating petals. Do this as many times as you desire for the flower you have in mind. Once all of your petals are laid down, use a standard tip to fill the center of your flower with a solid dot or multiple small ones.

Dahlias

Use a curved ribbon tip and create long petals fanning outward from the center and curving upward. Repeat layers of petals, each time getting slightly shorter and overlapping petals in previous layers. Fill the center with tiny dots using a standard tip.

Calla Lilies

Optionally, you can do two lilies at a time right next to each other and they can create a cute heart shape together. Begin with a petal tip with the narrow end faced upward. Create an upside-down teardrop shape with your piping, making a large petal that sticks out. Switch to your narrow standard tip with yellow buttercream and pipe a thin line inside of the shape you just created, which will make the lily's stamen. Go back to your petal tip and start piping at the very edge of your petal, creating the illusion that it's one seamless shape. As you "extend" this petal, pull toward the center of your lily and use that to cover the beginning of your stamen and the bottom of your first part of the petal. Repeat this step on the opposite side and overlap the other part of the petal you just did so that a wrap effect is created. If doing two lilies next to each other, create a heart effect by only doing this step for the outer edge of each lily and crossing all the way over to the center of both flowers, which will create a heart shape. Conceal the unfinished bottoms of your lilies with a couple of long leaves that reach up the sides and bend back down.

Lavender & Baby's Breath

Pipe a straight slightly curved line with a small standard tip and green buttercream. For lavender, use a similar tip to pipe small bulbs of frosting along each side that pull in toward the center. For baby's breath, add additional branches to your line first, then create medium sized circular bulbs with green and scatter them around the branches. Then use another plain tip to add white to the bulbs' centers.

Photo: Sian Elizabeth Siska, Sian Elizabeth Photography | www.sianelizabethphotos.com

You are a human "being,"
not a human "been."

Who you are now
and who you are
working to become is
profoundly more important
and will always outshine
who you used to be.

You are a constantly
evolving thing of
beauty, seeing the
passage of time and
deciding to grow along
with it, rather than resist.

The Relationship's Nutrition Label

Our relationships with others are complex, and a look at all the ingredients can help us work to improve the recipe.

Getting a degree in marriage and family therapy, I knew this was a question I would get all the time. "Is our relationship healthy?" "How is the relationship doing?" "Will we make it?" The irony in all of these questions is those people all have the power to know the answers to their questions way earlier than I do.

In addition, who am I to know what is and isn't healthy or beneficial for you? Granted, just like a nutrition label, there may be certain things where we can have a general and mutual understanding to some degree of whether or not something is probably good for us. However, other things are going to be up to the person for what that means. If you're trying to cut down sugar or salt, those quantities on the label might be really important for you. For me personally, I just turn to the part of the label that says "trans fat" and figure out some clever joke or pun to make about it as a plus size transgender person.

Even though many of the individual indicators in your relationships might be unique to your wants and needs, I suppose I can offer a couple great tools I know of that might be helpful hints if you're wanting to assess and improve your relationships.

5 Parts Sugar, 1 Part Salt

The first thing that would be a good indicator for how a relationship is doing is looking at a comprehensive view of how the interactions go in a relationship. In his research of couples, John Gottman studied the idea of a "magic ratio."

In this magic ratio, there was the understanding that every relationship has a ratio of positive to negative interactions. As you can likely deduce, a higher ratio of positive interactions to negative ones in your relationships is a good thing.

In his studies, Gottman noted that couples who were on the brink of divorce actually had ratios where the negative interactions were just slightly higher than positive. The recommended ratio for what he would consider a "healthy" relationship was about five positive interactions to every negative one, but couples could even strive to bring that five up to a seven or eight. What's important to note is that this may look different for everyone, so specifically trying to strive for a quota of compliments may end up doing more harm than good.

The biggest take away from all of this is to take the time to look at your relationships and see where the scales are tipped. If you're finding that there's more negative interactions in that balance than you'd like, think of creative but genuine ways to sprinkle more love and kindness into your relationship.

Source: Gottman, J. M., & Silver, N. (2015). *The seven principles for making marriage work*. New York: Harmony Books.

Sugar Coat That Criticism

It is absolutely vital that we find ways to communicate in our relationships that our needs aren't being met. Where we make a mess of things often is when we don't bring up concerns because we don't have the words to lovingly provide feedback and we end up holding it inside until we're too bothered to care and we let it spill out in a hot mess of anger.

One of the best things I've ever learned to avoid this mess and practice my ability to provide feedback and assert my needs in a loving way is nonviolent communication, which was introduced by the founder of the Center for Nonviolent Communication, Marshall Rosenberg. He also, like a surprising number of people who have been instrumental in developing tools and models used in therapy and counseling, was educated in Wisconsin. Total shameless plug there, woot woot.

The simplest way that I could explain nonviolent communication is this magical fill-in-the-blank format that allows you to communicate with your partner about what you're needing and giving them feedback. The four parts (or blanks) of nonviolent communication are observation, feeling, need, and request.

Observation: This is what you've seen or noticed that you're providing feedback on. Keep it literal and objective, don't put your own spins on it. The observation isn't that they've made you upset, it's things like not telling you that you're out of butter which makes you upset as a result.

Feeling: This is how that observation makes you feel. Once again, keep it literal and stick to your own feeling, not spinning it on them. It's not that you feel like they don't care, it's that you're feeling lonely or without support which hurts you.

Source: Rosenberg, M. B. (1999). Nonviolent communication: A language of compassion. Del Mar, CA: Puddle Dancer Press.

Need: With the observation you've stated and how it makes you feel, what need of yours is not getting met because of all of this. I cannot stress enough, don't put this on them and say something like "I need... you to do [insert chore here]." The need would be something more like "I need to feel a sense of peace and be free from chaos in my own home, which is hard when it's quite messy" or "I need to feel like we're both invested in our home together."

Request: Last but not least, what can you ask of them that may help this need be met? Keep it reasonable and open to compromise and negotiation. You want this to be a way they can actually help you have that need met, rather than set them up for failure.

When you put it all together, nonviolent communication looks a little something like this:

"When you [observation], I feel [feeling]. I need [need], so I'm wondering if you would be willing to [request]?"

For example: **"When you use the last of the butter and don't tell me we need more, I feel frustrated. I need to feel like the fridge is stocked especially when I have baking projects coming up, so I'm wondering if you can let me know next time we're out of butter?"**

See how kind and loving that was, but also directly stating what you're needing and wanting to see? It's so great!

Less Red Flags, More Red Velvet

One final slice of wisdom to be offered is watching out for red flags in your relationships. Many of us have probably heard this term. For those who don't know, these are those things within a relationship that might raise little alarms in our minds that something isn't quite right.

Before we jump right into hunting mode, a few caveats first: Most importantly, don't pressure yourself to spend every waking moment of your life on the lookout for these red flags in your relationships. Not only will you start to find ones that aren't there, but you'll also never find the emotional energy to see the really good things when they happen. The other thing that's important is to be kind and patient with yourself if you come to find that you have missed red flags that had been popping up before. As is said so eloquently in the Netflix adult animation series "Bojack Horseman" (which I would have never expected to quote in a cookbook): "When you look at someone through rose-colored glasses, all the red flags just look like flags."

The final thing that I feel the need to reiterate is that—like many things in relationships—there's probably some things that are generally understand and mutually agreed upon across relationships as red flags. However, many of the specific red flags will be dependent upon what you decide they are based on your own specific needs and perspectives. What you deem as indicators of unacceptable behavior, just like deeming what constitutes as unacceptable behavior in the first place, will be up to you to decide.

The other conversation I've seen recently around red flags that I think is important to mention is actually about the green flags in our lives and relationships. What are the really good things that instinctually make you realize that this is a great relationship. Most relationships will have both red and green flags, and neither of them are inherently prophetic about the success for failure of that relationship. Instead, think of them as conversation starters. Have a dialogue about those things you've noticed, both to prevent further negatives but also to reinforce and express appreciation for the things you find really good as well.

In ~~Confection~~ Conclusion

Just like a nutrition label, the best expert on whether or not your relationship is healthy for you and meeting your needs is going to be you at the end of the day. However, I hope that some of these tools will help strengthen your relationship so that you don't even have to worry about its nutrition label in the first place.

Part Three

LOVING
OUR WAY
FORWARD

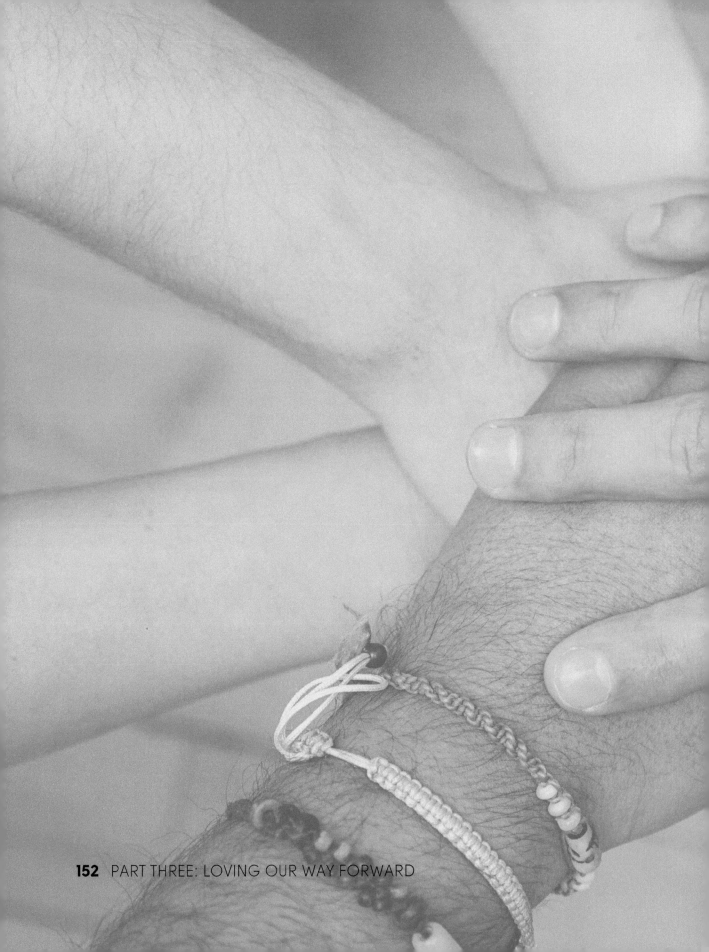

We are in the final part of this journey together. I'm so proud of the progress you have made thus far. Before we move forward, I have one small thing left for you to do from the previous section. As we've just spent all of that time talking about the relationships in our lives, and as you've thought about how those people make your life sweeter, I want you to do something.

Before you turn to the next page, I want you to put this book down for a moment and think of someone who you've recognized as one of those individuals who sweetens your life. Maybe it's a partner, or a friend, or a family member, or a neighbor, whoever it is. It might even be the case where a few different people pop up for you, and that's great. For those people that come to mind, take a second to let them know your appreciation. It could be a phone call, or a quick text, or a deep and profound video chat session until two in the morning. You can tell them this book told you to do it, or not. Either way is fine. You can come back to the book when you're done. I'll still be here.

How did that feel? I hope that it brightened your day a little bit, as well as theirs. Try and make moments like that a habit more often. I know I'll try to, so don't worry about being in it alone. We got this.

Many of the topics—as well as the recipes—in this final part of the book will be more complex than we've yet encountered. It may be challenging at times, but just know that I wholeheartedly believe in you. With many of these topics, we might surprise ourselves. They're not things that we're used to stopping to think about and be intentional with. But once we practice these things a few times, we can see how much of a powerful impact they can have on making the world a kinder, more thoughtful, and (most importantly) sweeter place for everyone around us.

How rare you are, being the only instance of yourself within a cosmic infinity.

The night sky is not made beautiful by any single, solitary star. Instead, by the glittering ensemble of countless celestial bodies.

Our unique experience is neither dulled nor tarnished by the reality that we each are just as cosmically rare as those around us.

A room of priceless treasures only becomes more valuable with each rare trinket until the only thing that sparkles more is the vast midnight sky draping over us.

Fave Flavors are Opinion, ~~Hate Isn't~~

Our lives are more complicated than chocolate or vanilla, so let's not impose our favorite flavor on others.

Let's break down the differences between an opinion versus a truth or reality. Many times, I think we find ourselves making the mistake of conflating these concepts and blurring them all together into a confusing mess.

Someone's opinion is their personal feeling on any given topic, whereas their truth and reality are the circumstances or contexts they find themselves in that may even inform those opinions.

Let's use an example here: one of my favorite cupcake recipes is lemon cheesecake. While I love all of my recipes, that one tastes the best for me with my specific taste preference. For my fiancé, his favorite flavor is chocolate chip. These are our opinions and they clearly differ, which is okay. Our truths and realities are that we each have the individual and unique taste buds that we do, as well as plenty of other contexts, that lead us to form that opinion.

I'm not going to turn to my fiancé and tell him that his opinion is wrong because my taste buds clearly tell me that lemon cheesecake is the most delicious. That would be ridiculous, and also incredibly disrespectful and invalidating of his feelings. My taste buds are the only accurate source for *my* opinions and they won't be accurate for his, so I can't impose the assumption that they would.

The problem that often comes up navigating these two different concepts is when we lump them together. Instead of recognizing opinion and truth/reality as separate concepts, we start having feelings that others' truths and realities are actually their opinions and thus can be disagreed with and up for debate.

As we've hit on several times now, our own truths and realities are ours, and no one else's. As such, we can't own each other's truths or modify them to what would make more sense for our own realities or truths. To love unconditionally is to accept truths as they are and see the value and beauty in them no matter how difficult, uncomfortable, painful, or how strongly they push against truths of our own.

But why do we do this? I believe a large contributor is that we live in a very individualist and black-and-white society. Between those two things, I feel that we've been conditioned to become very protective and territorial over our own truths and realities—which would totally make sense in most contexts—and we've also let black-and-white thinking influence us to believe that other truths that differ from our own pose a direct threat to the validity of our own realities that we've worked to protect.

I'm a firm believer in the both/and of things, and embracing that idea has been one of the most profound sources of my ability to grow in recent years. I hope that it can be helpful for you as well. Give yourself the permission to see multiple truths that exist simultaneously. Gift yourself the freedom and ease to not bear the weight and obligation of needing to decide.

In slowly beginning to embrace the complex and beautiful nature of the world and permitting ourselves to see multiple truths, we can start the process of demonstrating to our minds and hearts that the truths of others are not a threat to our own. Our bodies can begin to lower those guards that have been up for so long, preventing us from having more loving and understanding relationships with the world and her people. With a loving whisper and kind hand, we can tell the iron-clad gates that keep us from appreciating the rich diversity of the world, "Hi there, I appreciate you for trying to protect me, but I can take it from here. You can go rest now. Your work is done."

As we move forward in the world, practice expanding your capacity to see others' realities and try to not view it as opinion because you don't have the same truth. If you're not sure whether something expressed by someone is an opinion or their truth, err on the side of caution. It can't hurt.

There are many people in countless communities right now that are suffering because of their realities becoming warped into matters of opinion. As a queer person, my reality of loving outside of a heteronormative frame has been something that others have laid claim to having an opinion about. Even now, I find myself in a turbulent political time and wondering whether I will be able to fully and legally cement my relationship with the love of my life because others have made opinions of my reality. As a transgender and nonbinary person, I am constantly subjected to erasure, glares, mockery, and even threats of violence because others have formed opinions of my reality.

There are many other examples of realities I could list outside of my own experience that have been twisted into matters of opinion. This could include my friends and loved ones who are people of color, who are undocumented, or who practice a faith other than Christianity. I chose to use my own truths and realities as examples because I will never be able to intimately understand those truths that my loved ones hold. But the fact that I don't know is exactly the point.

The fact that I don't know the realities of people who hold different experiences than my own is the very reason I need to embrace those realities as valid and true. The fact is that we're the expert on our own realities and experiences, and we will never be the expert for someone else's. Hear what the expert has to say, and know that they probably know what they're talking about. There's no reason that we should deny someone's truth simply because we don't understand it. It's time that we hold more trust in people stating their truths and realities and acknowledge them because they're coming from the expert. This may seem like blind faith when we trust something we don't comprehend, but we do it all the time for way less important things. If you can accept the terms and conditions for your phone update without reading them, I think you can hold others' truths and realities as valid. And don't lie, none of us read those things before we click "update."

So then comes the question: What happens when someone inevitably is claiming opinion over someone's reality? You do the same thing you do when someone says their cupcakes are a secret family recipe, but you know the secret is that they hope no one noticed that clamshell grocery store packaging you saw in the trash can outside on your way to the front door. You kindly pull them aside and tell them that they can claim all they want but that doesn't make it true. You can have the opinion that grocery store baked goods are delicious, and many are! However, you can't assert that you've made them because it feels better than saying they were on sale and you were running late getting home from work. Just like how we can't claim an opinion on others' realities because it makes us more comfortable than addressing the hard truth that society has continued to make their lives harder and we benefit from that.

I also have absolutely zero doubt that addressing other's opinions and statements as harmful will be met with pushback. I get it all the time. The one I hear most often is about how I am supposed to expect people to respect my opinion (/existence) when I don't respect their opinion (/bias and discrimination). Then they usually finish with a rhetort of "I thought you preached tolerance!"

At this point they probably think they won this conversation. Knowing me, it's just like when I'm debating if I've gone too far with my garnishes: I'm just getting started.

Let's talk about a concept known as the paradox of tolerance. It was first introduced by philosopher Karl Popper. The paradox of tolerance implies that to be truly tolerant, you must be intolerant of intolerance itself.

Yes, I'm fully aware that the idea of being intolerant to be tolerant seems backwards and counter-intuitive, but trust me here. This paradox goes on to explain that intolerance itself is a very aggressive and active force. I'm sure we all can agree with that sentiment. Where it gets more intricate is that—if we live in a society that is truly 100% tolerant of absolutely everything—the intolerance's aggressive and active nature will allow it to stamp out the tolerance in that society. Therefore, a society that values tolerance can neither tolerate intolerance nor allow intolerance to spread and overpower tolerance in that society.

If we truly strive for a tolerant society, we must actively resist rhetoric that harms marginalized communities. This is also why we cannot have our refusal to accept hateful statements and "opinions" be distorted as no less intolerant as the intolerant statements themselves.

Passively allowing the persistence of discriminatory ideologies that harm marginalized communities so we don't feel "intolerant" is no less intolerant than declaring those sentiments ourselves.

Source: Popper, K. R., Ryan, A., & Gombrich, E. H. (2013). *The open society and its enemies.* Princeton: Princeton University Press.

Crème Brûlée

TAKE A CRACK AT IT

If you want to feel fancy, this cupcake is the way to go. Rich flavors, decadent filling, plus the beautiful contrast of the soft cake and the crunch of caramelized sugar.

Ingredients

CAKE
- 2 large eggs, separated
- 2 1/4 cups all-purpose flour
- 2 1/2 tsp. baking powder
- 1/2 tsp. salt
- 3/4 cup butter, softened
- 1 3/4 cups granulated sugar
- 3 tsp. pure vanilla extract
- 1 cup whole milk

FROSTING
- 1 cup softened butter
- 4 cups confectioner's sugar
- 3 tbsp. heavy cream or milk
- 2 tsp. pure vanilla extract
- 1/4 tsp. salt

FILLING & TOPPING
- 1 cup sugar + extra half cup for topping/garnish
- 3/4 cup all-purpose flour
- 3/4 tsp. salt
- 3 cups milk
- 3 egg yolks, whisked together
- 2 tbsp. butter
- 2 tsp. pure vanilla extract
- 1/2 cup heavy whipping cream

A hard shell to crack

You are a beautiful person with so much richness in your heart and soul. It makes sense to put up a shield to protect that good from others who may taint it, and you're entitled to those boundaries. Just make sure that shell isn't too hard, so that you can enjoy it and share it with those you love on your own terms.

Instructions

- If making your own fruit topping, make in advance.
- Preheat oven to 350°F and fill your cupcake tin with desired cupcake papers or liners. To get started on the cake, beat egg whites until soft peaks form then set aside. Sift flour, baking powder, and salt in another bowl and whisk together until combined.
- Cream butter then add sugar, mixing until well combined. Add egg yolks and vanilla and mix again.
- Add dry ingredients and whole milk to your mixture in portions, alternating between them and both starting and ending with the dry ingredients. After dry ingredients and milk are fully incorporated, gently fold in the whipped egg whites until smooth.
- Pour batter into baking cups until approximately 3/4 full and then bake approximately 18-21 minutes or until a toothpick comes out clean. Allow to cool.
- While cupcakes are baking, begin making filling by whipping cream until stiff peaks form and setting aside. Add sugar, flour, salt, and milk to a saucepan, adding the milk slowly as you mix until combined. Add yolks and bring mixture to a boil, stirring until a thicker consistency similar to pudding is achieved.
- Take off heat before adding butter and vanilla and mixing until combined and all butter has melted. Allow to cool before folding in your whipped cream and placing your filling in a piping bag.
- Make frosting by creaming butter before gradually adding confectioner's sugar until the desired consistency is reached. Add vanilla and salt for flavor. Thin with milk or cream as needed. Transfer to piping bag with desired tip.
- Assemble by removing the center of a cooled cupcake with a small knife or apple corer. Fill with filling. Pipe a swirl of frosting on top. Use sugar to garnish in one of the following ways: Sprinkle sugar on top of cupcakes and use a small torch to caramelize the exterior. You can also achieve a similar effect by placing sugared cupcakes in the broiler for a few seconds, although definition of frosting will melt leaving smooth domes. A final alternative would be to melt sugar before spreading on a flat cookie sheet and smashing once hardened to create decorative sugar shards.

Makes approximately 12-16 cupcakes.

Cake recipe adapted from Sally's Baking Addiction | www.sallysbakingaddiction.com
Filling recipe adapted from Happy Money Saver | www.happymoneysaver.com

Pink Champagne

BAKED BUBBLY BLISS

These cupcakes are a perfect celebratory treat. Whether you're ringing in the new year, celebrating a wedding or engagement, or just feel like living your best life with some cupcakes that'll make you feel real fancy, these cupcakes are a crystal clear winner. For a non-alcoholic version, use sparkling grape juice instead of the champage.

Ingredients

CAKE

- 1 1/2 cups all-purpose flour
- 1/2 tbsp. baking powder
- 1/4 tsp. salt
- 2 large eggs, room temperature
- 2/3 cup granulated sugar
- 3/4 cup melted butter
- 2 tsp. pure vanilla extract
- 1/2 cup milk
- 1 cup champagne, pink or otherwise
- 1-2 drops pink gel food coloring (optional)

FROSTING

- 1/2 cup butter, softened
- 3-5 cups confectioner's sugar
- 1/2 cup champagne, pink or otherwise
- 1-2 tbsp. heavy whipping cream
- 1 1/2 tsp. pure vanilla extract
- 1 tsp. pink gel food coloring, more or less for preferred shade

Cheers to that...

We really never celebrate enough, and living life is something to cheer for by itself! Think of something you could be celebrating right now. Even the lowest lows are merely the chance for us to move forward toward something bigger and better. Spend more time celebrating the little things.

Instructions

- Preheat oven to 350°F and fill your cupcake tin with desired cupcake papers or liners.
- Sift flour, baking powder, and salt into a medium bowl before whisking until combined.
- In another bowl, beat eggs and sugar together, gradually adding butter and vanilla. Beat until foamy and light.
- Add half of dry ingredients, then milk and champagne, then the remaining dry ingredients, mixing in between. If desired, add food coloring until batter is a delicate, light pink. Pour mixture into baking cups to about 3/4 full.
- Bake for 18-20 minutes until an inserted toothpick comes out clean. Allow to fully cool.
- While cupcakes are baking, make pink champagne frosting by creaming butter until smooth. Gradually add confectioner's sugar until close to the desired consistency. Add champagne and vanilla and mix well. Add additional confectioner's sugar to thicken or heavy whipping cream to thin as needed. Once the desired consistency is achieved, use food coloring to turn frosting your desired shade of pink.
- Fill a piping bag with frosting and decorate cooled cupcakes with it. Garnish with sugar pearls or edible flowers.

Makes approximately one dozen cupcakes

One of our most magical talents is the ability to see the world around us and make meaning of it all as we take in its beauty.

To find the good in what we see before us is a deeply powerful force for creating a more loving world than the one we were given.

Don't Judge a Cupcake by its Paper

Cupcakes can look great in a fancy package, but good "taste" doesn't mean it tastes good.

This is one of those kindergarten lessons we hear time and time again. Even though we've heard it so many times, it appears to be a lesson we're constantly needing reminders for. This age-old lesson, for many of us, is a bit more complicated than we originally had thought.

The way that this issue shows up for a lot of us is through implicit bias. Whereas something like discrimination or prejudice would be the more explicit actions or beliefs based on pre-determined factors, implicit bias is... well... more implicit. It's the subtle and almost instinctual reactions that are so deep we don't even realize that they're happening. If we do catch them, it's after they've already begun.

What do some of these implicit biases look like? One of the most prevalent ways that they show up is in the form of implicit racism. What are some of those snap judgements you find yourself making in the moment when you interact with various people of color? Perhaps it's locking your car door when a black man walks by, or maybe it's the nearly instant reaction of wondering if they're undocumented when you hear a brown person speaking a language other than your own.

The part that's so insidious about these implicit biases we hold is that they're so subtle that we barely notice them. And yet, they have the profound ability to impact the lives of those whom which these biases are held against. Locking the car door is one thing, but what happens when it's those same implicit biases when you're the loan manager and this man is hoping to get an affordable mortgage for a home for him and his family?

These biases exist within us and people of marginalized communities pay the price at every turn in their lives. If we are to address these biases, we must recognize that this isn't their issue with which we empathize, but our issue that we must solve.

Many of us fail to address the biases within us because it's incredibly uncomfortable—and perhaps even painful. Things like racism are shown to us as children in very sensationalized ways. We see imagery of slavery, segregation, and white supremacist groups, but we don't see the implicitly racist banker or hiring authority. While those sensationalized lenses can definitely deter some of the more explicit forms of discrimination in our minds, it also creates this feeling of exaggerated shame and discomfort around racism that prevents us from even exploring the most subtle biases we have in our hearts.

When difficult topics like racism, sexism, homophobia, cisgenderism, classism, or ableism come up in conversation, our first and most immediate response is to prove that we're not the problem, offering the remark of "I'm not racist" or "I don't have anything against gay people," or "I treat everyone equally," as efficiently as we possibly can. It's the instinctual fire alarm in our bodies to put out the red-hot discomfort burning up inside us like the world depends upon it.

The irony is that, in jumping as quick as we can to prove that we're not racist or sexist or homophobic or have whatever other possible bias, we actually end up perpetuating those exact same structures of oppression that we claim to have no part of. In rushing to declare our innocence or decry any involvement, we establish that our comfort is a higher priority than having meaningful but hard conversations that work toward healing the wounds of discrimination and systemic violence.

Besides the fact that we reinforce the very things we're trying to deny in those sentiments, the other glaring issue is that those statements are entirely false. We live in an environment that continues to marginalize communities of color, queer and transgender communities, impoverished communities, and so many more. We've grown up with the teachings of that very same society and we've trained for years to be skilled in covert bias, even if those same teachings attempted to condemn the more explicit forms of discrimination and bigotry. Our biases have been reinforced over decades of stereotype, lack of representation, and re-tellings of history that have been designed to benefit oppressive systems by portraying them in sanitized and generously positive lights.

Communities are wounded and we can no longer choose to resist coming in to help because we're uneasy with the sight of blood. We can no longer be selfish and decide that our comfort is more important than these communities' right to peace and safety. Instead of quickly jumping at the opportunity to deny our involvement in racism and other forms of discrimination, we need to acknowledge that this society has some work to do and that as members of that society, that means us too. It's profoundly easier—as well as kinder to ourselves and those around us—to admit that we're a work in progress and commit to growth, rather than performing the mental gymnastics trying to convince ourselves otherwise because that's what feels safer.

We owe it to ourselves and others to acknowledge our existence as works in progress. We would never take cupcakes out of the oven knowing they're still raw inside and serve them while hoping that everyone will just understand. No! Absolutely not! You put those babies back in until they're ready. So why would we decide to cut ourselves short on our chance to grow as people? What's even better is the beautiful difference between us and cupcakes where we will be able to always keep growing and we won't dry out or even burn like cupcakes would if they stayed in the oven too long. We can have a lifetime's worth of growth, so why stop?

This will be a long journey, but I promise that it is worth it. It may be painful at times to see and acknowledge our own biases, but it will be significantly kinder to ourselves and others in the long run if we see it as it is and work to grow. Something profound I heard years ago that may be helpful in this work is, "Our first thought defines our background, but our second thought defines our character." This is the most important part of this work.

You won't always be able to determine what that first thought is. You may live the rest of your life and find that you still have some biases that you were never able to quite unlearn. But you have much more power over that second thought. The choice will be yours now of what that second thought could be. Will it be one that strives to deny and bury the first? Or will it be one that acknowledges our areas for growth and improvement and commits to progressing forward anyway? You deserve the chance to keep growing, give yourself the permission.

Orange Creamsicle

ORANGE YOU GLAD TO SEE THIS RECIPE?

This summer treat is about to become your main squeeze. Inspired by the just-as-delicious popsicle flavor, this fun cupcake is an equal mix of both sweet and refreshing.

Ingredients

CAKE

- 2 cups all-purpose flour
- 1 1/2 tsp. baking powder
- 1/2 tsp. baking soda
- 1 tsp. salt
- 10 tbsp. butter, room temperature
- 1 1/4 cups granulated sugar
- 3 large eggs
- 1 tsp. vanilla extract
- 2/3 cup milk
- 3 tbsp. grated orange zest
- 1/4 cup fresh orange juice
- 1 tsp. orange gel food coloring

FROSTING

- 1/2 cup butter, softened
- 3-4 cups confectioner's sugar
- 1 tbsp. pure vanilla extract
- 1-2 tbsp. heavy whipping cream
- 1 tsp. orange zest

FILLING & TOPPING

- 2 cups heavy whipping cream
- 1/3 cup granulated sugar
- 2 tsp. pure vanilla extract
- 6 popsicle sticks (for garnish, optional)

Enjoy the fruit of your labors...

Try not to mistake confidence for arrogance. It isn't arrogant to acknowledge your successes and be proud of yourself for them. Don't deny yourself the tangible rewards of your hard work. You deserve them, and you should be proud.

Instructions

- Preheat oven to 350°F and fill your cupcake tin with desired cupcake papers or liners.
- To get started on the cake, sift your dry ingredients: flour, baking powder, baking soda, and salt, and whisk together until well combined.
- Cream butter before adding sugar with a hand or stand mixer. When combined, add one egg and mix again, continuing with the remaining eggs one at a time. Add vanilla and orange zest.
- Add 1/3 of the dry ingredients to the mixer and combine. Then follow with half of the milk and orange juice and combine. Repeat so the order of adding to the mix is dry, liquid, dry, liquid, dry. When finally combined, add orange food coloring until you reach a desirable shade.
- Pour batter into baking cups until approximately 3/4 full and then bake approximately 35 minutes or until an inserted toothpick comes out clean.
- While cupcakes are baking, begin making filling by whipping cream until stiff peaks form. Mix in sugar and vanilla, combining well. Set aside.
- Make frosting by creaming butter together before gradually adding confectioner's sugar until the desired consistency is reached. Add vanilla and orange zest for flavor. Thin with milk or cream as needed. Transfer to piping bag with desired tip.
- Assemble by removing the center of a cooled cupcake with a small knife or apple corer. Fill with filling. Pipe frosting on your cupcake and finish by garnishing with additional zest and/or with half of a popsicle stick.

Makes approximately one dozen cupcakes.

Summer Sparkler

A SPARK OF GENIUS

When someone proposed this cupcake idea to me, I thought they were ridiculous. What blew my mind even more was when I tasted one of these for the first time. When my friend and I were trying these, we were beyond words. All of the flavors were there, and it even somehow still had the popsicle vibes that we couldn't quite put our finger on. All of the childhood nostalgia and more. Try it for yourself.

Ingredients

CAKE

- 1 1/2 cups all-purpose flour
- 1/2 tbsp. baking powder
- 1/4 tsp. salt
- 2 large eggs, room temperature
- 2/3 cups granulated sugar
- 3/4 cup melted butter
- 1 tsp. pure vanilla extract
- 1/2 cup milk
- 1 tsp. lemon zest
- Juice and zest of 1-2 limes
- 2 tsp. raspberry extract
- 1 tbsp. juice from a jar of maraschino cherries
- Several drops each of red and blue food coloring

FROSTING

- 1 cup butter, softened
- 4-6 cups powdered sugar
- 1 tbsp. heavy whipping cream
- 1-2 tbsp. each of cherry, lime, and raspberry flavor syrups
- 1 tsp. lemon juice
- Several drops each of red and blue food coloring

Never dull your sparkle...

You bring so much light into the world and it's a more beautiful place with you in it. Don't let anyone ever tell you otherwise. Got it?

Instructions

- Preheat oven to 350°F and fill your cupcake tin with desired cupcake papers or liners.
- Sift flour, baking powder, and salt into a medium bowl before whisking until combined.
- In another bowl, beat eggs and sugar together, gradually adding butter and vanilla. Beat until foamy and light.
- Add half of dry ingredients, then milk, then the remaining dry ingredients, mixing in between.
- Split mixture evenly among three bowls. In one bowl, mix in raspberry extract, lemon zest, and blue food coloring. In another bowl, mix in lime juice and zest. In the final bowl, add cherry juice and red food coloring.
- Carefully spoon or pipe each color one at a time into your baking cups, starting with red, then white, then blue on top. Being slow and gentle with this step will allow for more defined layers and prevent batter from sinking when you add it.
- Bake for 18-20 minutes until an inserted toothpick comes out clean. Allow to fully cool.
- While cupcakes are baking, make frosting by creaming together butter before gradually adding powdered sugar until the desired consistency. Because of the syrups that will be added, you may want to go for slightly stiffer than usual as the extra liquid will thin it out. Similar to the batter, separate mixture evenly among three bowls. In one bowl, add cherry flavor to taste and red food coloring. In another bowl, add lime flavoring to taste. In the final bowl, add raspberry flavoring and lemon juice to taste, as well as blue food coloring.
- Spread all three frostings in a row alongside each other on a sheet of plastic wrap. Roll the plastic wrap into a red, white, and blue tube and insert into a piping bag. Pipe some excess frosting out onto a plate or other surface to get all three colors going. Pipe onto fully cooled cupcakes. Garnish with red, white, and blue sprinkles, half of a popsicle stick or a sparkler candle.

Makes approximately one dozen cupcakes

Our ability to work together with love in our hearts and passion in our souls is what will move humanity forward.

We cannot do this alone.

As the saying goes, "build a longer table, not a taller fence."

Not Everyone has a Dishwasher

We can't assume we bake the same when everyone has a different kitchen.

Hi, allow me to introduce myself. My name is "not everyone." It's me. I don't have a dishwasher. Never have, and so desperately hoping to someday live that dream. How I hope to one day be able to just stock a rack and let that bad boy take care of it all for me while I enjoy a nice after-dinner glass of wine. In the meantime though, it's still washing by hand for me.

A dishwasher is but one of many kitchen innovations that can make life so much easier, especially when you bake as much as I do. Another fabulous invention would be the stand mixer. I recently got one as a present from my future mother-in-law for getting my Master's Degree. I knew a stand mixer would be pretty helpful but SWEET JESUS I had no idea how magical they were and how much easier life was with one. The first time I could leave heavy cream all by its bad self to whip and aerate while I went to go work on something else was entirely life-changing.

The point of this isn't to brag or have a whisk-measuring contest about who has what in their kitchens. We all will have different things in our kitchens, as well as components of the kitchens themselves, that will make our own individual baking experiences vastly different and unique to each of us.

The plot twist here is that the things making our lives easier or harder go way beyond the walls of our kitchens. Let's talk about a little thing called privilege.

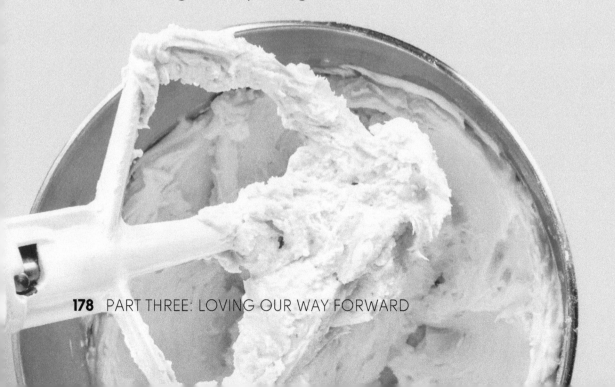

Privilege is the unearned advantages that we get in life because of various different factors like our identities or status. These unearned advantages get taken for granted while other groups are denied them. Despite these advantages not existing across the board for everyone, they quickly become defined as the norm and it's expected that everyone has them. It's not necessarily that these advantages should be taken away, especially as many of them actually tend to look more like basic human rights. The goal is actually that we should be improving the society and communities we live in so that everyone can experience those benefits and advantages.

For example, a privilege that I do not have as a transgender and nonbinary person is the privilege to be able to walk into a public building and automatically expect that there will be a bathroom option for me. In addition to there being a bathroom at all, I would be able to know that I can use it safely, and should not have any reasonable fear of harassment, glares, or even threats of violence if I decide to use it. Cisgender people have that privilege most of the time, but I don't. One privilege I do have as a white person is that I can go into a store, decide that they didn't have what I was looking for, and walk out empty-handed without a worry that I'll be suspected of shoplifting. Many people of color don't have that luxury. In fact, not only are they suspected of shoplifting when they leave empty-handed, but many people of color are often followed as they walk through the store because people already anticipate that they will attempt to steal something. As a white person, I have the privilege of benefit-of-the-doubt, and my simple existence isn't assumed to be criminal.

I would strongly encourage you to do some online browsing around the idea of privilege. Many websites have tools like privilege checklists where you can go through a comprehensive list of various privileges to see how many of those advantages you have. It isn't so much about some competitive analysis to see if you're more or less privileged. What's powerful in that experience is just to simply see all of the different ways privilege exists that you had never even remotely thought of. We all have various privileges, and there are also privileges that we don't have. It's important that we're conscious of those things, especially so that we don't take our privileges for granted or expect that they're the standard for everyone.

So what do we do with this information? First of all, no one is asking you to apologize for having privilege. In addition, no one is saying that having privilege means that everything has been handed to you all of your life without work. Having privilege only means that your efforts in life aren't met with extra work and the work you do is met with higher chances of success. Rather than getting defensive or feeling the need to apologize, what you can do about your privilege is just be aware of it.

If you find out that your friend doesn't have a dishwasher or a stand mixer when you do, you don't apologize for that or get defensive either. What's important for you to do instead is be mindful of the privileges you have and not try to make someone else's lack of privilege any worse. You don't have dinner at a friend's house and decide to recklessly stockpile dirty dishes on them and say something like "it's not that much. It'll probably only be one cycle in the... oh wait... that's right! You don't have a dishwasher. So sorry about that! Maybe you should just bite the bullet and get one!" Sure, I'll get on that ASAP with this empty wallet, student debt, and this rental property that I don't own.

In addition to just being mindful of your privileges and not imposing the same standards on those without, you can also be on the lookout for little ways that you can close the gap for them. Sometimes closing that gap may just be a helping hand and it may even include using some of your own privileges strategically. Instead of that first scenario, what if it was something different like "Hey, that's a lot of dishes to do by hand. Can I help you so you're not stuck doing them all night? Then we might even have time to watch that great movie you were telling me about over dinner!"

It doesn't have to be some grand gesture—it can be those little things where you just offer a hand to make their life a little bit easier when life has given them an obstacle. Our ability to lend a hand to each other is one of the most profound gifts that I think we have as human beings. Let's use it.

Tiramisù

LAYERED WITH LOVE

We did it y'all. This the last recipe in the book *cue sad violin music as you say "Awwww" and dramatically reach for the tissues. As the last recipe in the book, I can also honestly say this is one of the recipes I'm most proud of. It took an immense amount of trial and error, but it was worth it. Even having it all figured out now, she's still a labor of love. I hope you'll love these cupcakes like I do.

Ingredients

CAKE

- 1 batch vanilla cake batter, set aside (see pg. 66)
- 1 1/3 cup all-purpose flour
- 1/3 cup cocoa powder (plus a little extra for garnish)
- 1 tsp. baking powder
- 1/2 tsp. baking soda
- 1/4 tsp. salt
- 1/2 cup whole milk
- 1/2 cup strong brewed coffee
- 2 tsp. espresso powder
- 1 tsp. pure vanilla extract
- 1/2 cup butter, softened
- 1/2 cup each, granulated & brown sugar
- 1 egg, room temperature

FROSTINGS

- 1/2 cup butter, softened
- 2 cups confectioner's sugar
- 2 tbsp. granulated sugar
- 2 tsp. vanilla (1 tsp. for each)
- 1 1/2 tsp. espresso powder
- 1 cup heavy whipping cream
- 4 oz. mascarpone cheese (or cream cheese in a pinch)
- Brown gel food coloring (optional)

"Espress"ing my gratitude...

I can't even begin to describe how thankful I am for you being on this journey with me of spreading love and making the world a sweeter place. You are a gift to the world.

Instructions

- Preheat oven to 350°F and fill your cupcake tin with desired cupcake papers or liners.
- Make one batch of vanilla cupcake batter, according to instructions on page 66. Set batter aside. Begin espresso cake by adding espresso powder to brewed coffee. Mix until dissolved and set aside to cool to room temperature.
- Whisk together flour, cocoa, baking powder, baking soda, and salt. In another bowl, cream together butter, sugar, and brown sugar until fluffy. Add egg then mix again.
- Combine milk, coffee mixture, and vanilla in a small bowl or measuring cup. Add half of dry ingredients to batter, then the liquid mixture, and end with the remaining dry ingredients. Mix after each addition until well combined. Put vanilla cake batter and espresso cake batter into separate piping bags.
- Pipe thin layers batter into baking cups, alternating between vanilla and espresso batters, until approximately 3/4 full and then bake approximately 18-21 minutes or until a toothpick comes out clean. Allow to cool completely.
- While cupcakes are baking, combine heavy whipping cream, mascarpone/cream cheese, and 1 tsp. of vanilla to a bowl, beating until smooth. Slowly add sugar and continue to mix until stiff peaks form.
- In another bowl, cream butter together before gradually adding powdered sugar until the desired consistency is reached. Add espresso powder to the other tsp. of vanilla and mix until combined. Add vanilla and espresso mixture to the frosting and mix well. Color a darker shade of brown to contrast the mascarpone frosting (optional).
- Assemble a piping bag and fill one side with mascarpone frosting and the other side with espresso frosting. Pipe a small amount on a plate to get both frostings to start piping. Pipe a swirl of mascarpone and espresso frostings on cooled cupcakes before finishing off with a dusting of cocoa powder. Optionally garnish with edible gold leaf.

Makes approximately 24 cupcakes.

Espresso cake recipe adapted from Michelle Harris | www.justapinch.com

You are the most important ingredient to a sweeter world.

Sprinkle kindness everywhere you go.

Spread love like smooth buttercream.

Love Each Other, Lend Some Sugar

The power to make the world a sweeter place is within you now. Go forth and sprinkle.

What a beautiful and unique moment that we find ourselves in now. Breathe. Take it in. This magical moment is both the end and the beginning. How truly special.

As we find ourselves approaching the conclusion of this journey together, reflect on where and who you were when you first began. What has changed, if anything? What have you gained or learned that you are excited to take with you? Is there anything you would tell that past self that you know now and wished they had known coming into it? What thoughts are you looking to share with those in your life that you want to bring forward from this journey? Just as important as where you've come from in this journey is where you plan to go. What's next for you? How do you plan to make the world a sweeter place?

The work will not be done in our time together. In fact, I don't believe the work will ever be done as there will always be more ways to leave the world better than it was before. But that is all the more reason to keep going. In my opinion, the moment we stop learning and loving is the moment we stop living.

While I'm sure that there have been individual moments for you throughout this journey that have been profound revelations, I also recognize the likelihood that many of these things may not have been groundbreaking for you. That's okay. Sometimes the most helpful things are the gentle reminders of what we already knew. Moving forward, those reminders will always continue to be helpful as we mere mortals are constantly reminded of our inconsistencies and imperfections. Even in writing this book, there have been plenty of times where I've felt as though I've fallen off the tracks and gone against my own words. We're human. We do that sometimes.

Groundbreaking or not, you have everything in you to positively contribute to the world. You have the power to go out into the world and work toward fostering love and kindness everywhere you go. What a mighty gift you have. And remember, the conversations we've had throughout our time together may have watered the soil, but the seeds had been there all along.

Now, go forth and do your thing. The world is a sweeter place with you in it, and it's only going to get sweeter as you move forward from here. But, before you go, one more thing...

Thank you.

I profoundly appreciate you sharing your time and heart with me. Your vulnerability and strength are precious treasures, and I do not take this moment for granted. Even if we've never met, I have immense love for you and am forever thankful for the ways you make the world a sweeter place.

Move Forward with Love.

Let's end this intimate journey together with one final reminder, as painted so beautifully by my dear friend, Lindsey.

YOU ARE STRONG.
YOU ARE BEAUTIFUL.
YOU ARE
ENOUGH.

189

Painting: Lindsey Cherek Waller | www.lindseycherek.com

Surprise! Bonus Recipe!

"One pod, many beans...

Always remember that you're not alone. There's so many people in your corner that you may not even realize, and you are part of a beautiful community. If you still think no one is there for you, put me on the list.

"Cocoa Wacky Cake"
COMMUNITY IS THE SWEETEST

This recipe was gifted to me by a dear friend in my community, Mary. She is the premier example of someone who has led with love all of her life and who values her community. When I am older, I hope to be even half of the person and community member that Mary is. She kindly volunteered to use her years of experience in commercial baking to look over sections of this book for me, and she also raised one of the other coolest women I know, Sarah (who I mentioned earlier in the book).

Mary reminds me that love isn't always the grandeur and extravagance, and that sometimes the simplest gestures are the most powerful. Similarly, this recipe is so simple but so effective, which explains its ability to stand the test of time. It's also a recipe that many more people would be able to enjoy compared to a more standard recipe. When she gave it to me, Mary said, "This is the original recipe I got almost 48 years ago from a woman at 'The Farm' which was a commune. They were strictly vegan, heavy on all things soy, and big on lots of sugar. It's a very forgiving and adaptable recipe."

Ingredients

- 2 cups all-purpose flour
- 1 1/2 cups granulated sugar
- 1/3 cup cocoa
- 1 tsp. salt
- 1 tsp. baking soda
- 1 cup water
- 1 tbsp. vinegar
- 1 tsp. pure vanilla extract
- 1/2 cup oil

Instructions

- Preheat oven to 350°F and grease an 8-inch square or circle pan, or line a cupcake tin with papers of your choosing.
- Sift dry ingredients into a bowl and combine well. Set aside.
- Mix wet ingredients in a separate bowl and add to dry ingredients.
- Pour batter into pan or cupcake papers.
- Bake for approximately 25-30 minutes, until an inserted toothpick comes out clean.

Makes 1 8-inch cake or approximately one dozen cupcakes.
For layer cake, double recipe.

Recipe Courtesy of Mary Marin

References

Chapman, G. D. (1995). *The five love languages: How to express heartfelt commitment to your mate.* Chicago: Northfield Pub.

Clance, P. R., & Imes, S. A. (1978). The imposter phenomenon in high achieving women: Dynamics and therapeutic intervention. Psychotherapy: Theory, Research & Practice, 15(3), 241–247. https://doi.org/10.1037/h0086006

Gottman, J. M., & Silver, N. (2015). *The seven principles for making marriage work.* New York: Harmony Books.

Leach, B. (1975). *Living sober.* Alcoholics Anonymous World Services.

Popper, K. R., Ryan, A., & Gombrich, E. H. (2013). *The open society and its enemies.* Princeton: Princeton University Press.

Rosenberg, M. B. (1999). *Nonviolent communication: A language of compassion.* Del Mar, CA: Puddle Dancer Press.

Twist, M.L.C. (n.d.). "H.A.L.T.O. checklist." University of Wisconsin-Stout, Fall 2018. Class handout.

Recommended Additional Readings

Maybe You Should Talk to Someone: A Therapist, Her Therapist, and Our Lives Revealed
by Lori Gottlieb

How to Be You: Stop Trying to Be Someone Else and Start Living Your Life
by Jeffrey Marsh

My Grandmother's Hands: Racialized Trauma and the Pathway to Mending Our Hearts and Bodies
by Resmaa Menakem

Sissy: A Coming-of-Gender Story
by Jacob Tobia

Untamed
by Glennon Doyle

Today Means Amen
Poems by Sierra DeMulder

Over the Top: A Raw Journey to Self-Love
by Jonathan Van Ness

If My Body Could Speak
by Blythe Baird

Shame is an Ocean I Swim Across
Poems by Mary Lambert

This is Just My Face: Try Not to Stare
by Gabourey Sidibe

Cravings: Recipes for All the Food You Want to Eat and *Cravings: Hungry for More*
by Chrissy Teigen

You Deserve Love & Support

Here are some additional resources that might be helpful if you need a little extra love. Whether something was brought to your attention through this book, or something in your life started the conversation, there is no shame in reaching out for some extra help. If we weren't here to help each other, we wouldn't make it through this little thing we call life. Please use any of these if you need them, and I've included the up-to-date phone numbers or websites at the time of writing this. This also isn't an exhaustive list.

National Suicide Prevention Lifeline
800-273-8255 | suicidepreventionlifeline.org

The Trevor Project LGBTQIA+ Youth Suicide Hotline
1-866-488-7386 | thetrevorproject.org

Trans Lifeline
877-565-8860 | translifeline.org

NAMI: National Alliance on Mental Illness
nami.org

RAINN: Rape Abuse & Incest National Network
National Sexual Assault Hotline: 800-656-HOPE(4673) | rainn.org

Crisis Text Line
Text "HELLO" to 741741

SAMHSA: Substance Abuse and Mental Health Services Administration
National Helpline: 1-800-662-HELP (4357) | samhsa.gov/find-help

Directories for Finding a Therapist or Counselor
locator.apa.org | psychologytoday.com/us/therapists

About the Author & Contributor

COLTAN J. SCHOENIKE, MS
they, them, theirs

Coltan holds a Bachelor's Degree in Human Development and Family Studies with a concentration in LGBTQIA+ Studies & Education, a Master's Degree in Marriage & Family Therapy, and a Graduate Certificate in Sex Therapy from the University of Wisconsin-Stout in Menomonie, WI. As a queer and nonbinary person, they make it a professional and personal aspiration to do everything in their power to make the world a better place for all. With the recent completion of their Master's Degree, Coltan is currently working with the State of Wisconsin to obtain training licensure to practice supervised therapy and pursue certification as a Licensed Marriage & Family Therapist.

MARIA CAULEY, MS
she, her, hers

Maria completed her undergraduate degree, graduate degree, and dietetic internship through the University of Wisconsin - Stout in Menomonie, Wisconsin. Her professional passions include deconstructing diet culture, increasing diversity and inclusion in the dietetics profession, addressing systemic classism and racism, and decreasing food insecurity. Maria is currently in the final steps of the process for obtaining her certification as a Registered Dietitian.

Follow Maria's professional journey as a Registered Dietitian on Instagram @cauleyflower_nutrition

CPSIA information can be obtained
at www.ICGtesting.com
Printed in the USA
LVHW072010041220
673096LV00031B/611